Sutherland
An Illustrated Architectural Guide

IT GIVES ME GREAT PLEASURE to see the publication of Sutherland: An Illustrated Architectural Guide; and I am honoured to be asked to write its foreword.

Sutherland, the South-land of the Vikings (but hardly for anyone else) is the only historic county in Scotland which does not have a large town. (I may add that it is the only one to have no less than three coasts: west, north and east.) Its population has never amounted to more than a few tens of thousands. But this does not mean that there are not many buildings of interest and beauty characteristic of life through the centuries. Above all, there is Dornoch, with its cathedral and surrounding houses: a former royal burgh until the recent changes, although no more than a large village, lying beside a championship golf-course.

We who love our county very much hope that this guide to its buildings will help visitors to Sutherland to enjoy more than the scenery and to imagine the history of this still remote part of Scotland.

Elizabeth Sutherland

ELIZABETH SUTHERLAND
Countess of Sutherland
Chief of Clan Sutherland

© Author: Elizabeth Beaton
Series editor: Charles McKean
Series consultant: David Walker
Editorial consultant: Duncan McAra
Cover design: Dorothy Steedman, Almond Design
Index: Oula Jones

From Eric Rydehalgh.
29/7/98

The Rutland Press
ISBN 1 873190 24 7
1st published 1995

Cover illustrations
Front: Fanagmore, Loch Laxford (Sutherland Tourist Board)
Back: Top left Dornoch Post Office (RIAS Collection)
Bottom left Ardvreck Castle, Assynt (RIAS Collection)
Top right Balnakeil Church (RIAS Collection)
Middle right St Andrew's Church, Golspie (Beaton)
Bottom right Helmsdale harbour (Leet)

Typesetting and picture scans by Almond Design, Edinburgh
Printed by Nimmos Colour Printers, Edinburgh

Sutherland occupies about one-eighth of the land mass of Scotland. Bounded on the south by the Dornoch Firth, Strathcarron and Strath Oykel; to the north by the Pentland Firth separating the mainland from Orkney and on the west by the Atlantic Ocean and the North Minch. The most fertile land is in the east, falling away from the hills as a green coastal swathe. There are immense tracts of bare moorland in the central uplands while the west boasts outstanding landscapes of steep mountains and deeply indented coastline with bays and headlands. This northern territory is scattered with lochs, both large and small and bisected by river valleys which provide routes for railway and road, the latter usually single track with passing places. The broader valley bottoms contain isolated farms or shooting lodges; birch woods border the patches of arable land, sheltered by hills.

This contrasting rural landscape has a long settlement history. Archaeologists have identified hill forts, souterrains, burial sites and other evidence of prehistoric human habitation. Brochs occupy dominant sites overlooking valley and coast.

The archaeology of the recent past, particularly the 19th century, is visible to all. The remains of such townships as Rosal and Achinlochy in Strathnaver, of empty straths *cleared* of population for replacement by large sheep farms in the early 19th century, of linear crofts of strip fields running down to the

Beaton

Hill fort, Baligil on the rugged Pentland Firth coast: lime kiln in foreground

Opposite *Interior, Dornoch Cathedral*

Dun Dorndilla broch

RCAHMS

Wrought-iron cat, the crest of the Earls of Sutherland, as balustrade finial in old tower, Dunrobin Castle

Highland churches and manses: Thomas Telford drawings

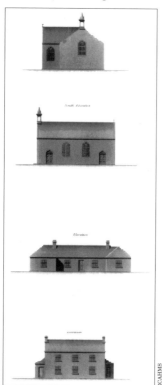

seashore or riverbank and of random coastal settlements with diminutive patches of arable land characterise the north and west. Large farms and greater population concentrate on the more prosperous east coast.

Scandinavian names reveal a former Nordic presence, the Gaelic ones a reminder that this was the principal language until recently. Historically, two families have dominated Sutherland. The Mackay Lords of Reay, together with lesser members of that family, were the hereditary landowners in the north-west, their importance reflected in handsome dwellings at Balnakeil, Tongue and Bighouse. The Freskynes (who became Gordons by marriage) were established by the 13th century in the east at Dunrobin, as Earls, later Dukes, of Sutherland: by 1830 they owned most of the county, including former Mackay territory. It is this family who has left, most evidently and distinctively, its mark on the built history of Sutherland.

Most early churches and burial grounds are sited near the coast, for the convenience of sea transport. The most important ecclesiastical building is Dornoch Cathedral on the northern shores of the Dornoch Firth. Dornoch is the principal town of Sutherland and the administration of the district is carried on from there and Golspie.

In Sutherland there was a substantial rebuilding of parish churches by Sir Robert Gordon (see p.29) in the early 17th century. Of these two survive at Balnakeil and Tongue, both unusually with centre doors and flanking windows in the long south elevations of the customary simple masonry rectangle.

It was the increased population in the vast Highland parishes, which led to the 1823 Act for Building Additional Places of Worship in the Highlands & Islands of Scotland furnishing £50,000 with which to provide both church and manse at 40 different sites. The Commission for Highland Roads & Bridges administered the project: its principal engineer, Thomas Telford, was responsible for designs for a church and alternative manses – one single, one two-storey – to cost not more than £1500 together excluding land. Though rightly ascribed to Thomas Telford, for his was the final responsibility, credit must also go to his assistants William Thomson and John Mitchell (d.1824), as well as James Smith, an Inverness builder. In Sutherland there are examples at

4

RCAHMS

Croick, Strathy and Stoer.
The discontent within the Church of Scotland in the mid-19th century is difficult to comprehend over a hundred years later in a more secular age. Sufficient that the vexed subject of patronage and choice of minister came to a head in 1843 when the *Disruption* tore the Church apart, most particularly in the Highlands where the greater proportion of the ministers *came out*, abandoning church, manse and security. They worshipped with large supportive congregations in barns and caves or in the open air, those congregations building and financing new Free churches and manses in an extraordinarily short time. Further schisms in 1892 and 1900 resulted in the establishment of the Free Presbyterian and United Free Churches. After a House of Lords judgement in 1904, re-allocating churches, the UF embarked on yet another round of church and manse building, many to become Church of Scotland property after the Union in 1929.

This somewhat complex church history accounts for a superabundance of ecclesiastical buildings, which can be understood only within the context of 19th- and 20th-century Scottish church history. Many are notable for their magisterial pulpits, monumental fittings dignifying otherwise plain interiors and exemplifying the importance of the sermon preached by generations of ministers, often with considerable oratory in both English and Gaelic.

The attempt to apply the *rationale* behind the Industrial Revolution in north-west England to the reorganisation of remote Sutherland in the first two decades of the 19th century, by relocating people with little or no

Beaton

Top *Stoer Parliamentary Church, in the isolated, rocky Assynt, 1829.*
Above *Migdale Free Church of Scotland*

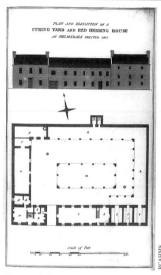

Plan and elevation, curing yard, Helmsdale, 1817, from James Loch, An Improvement on the Estate of the Marquess of Stafford (1820), designed by George Alexander

Big Barns: 18th-century barn near Dunrobin converted to four cottages by George Devey, 1858

English, who exercised a barely self-sufficient economy and who as *kindly tenants* for generations considered their ancestral land tenure inviolable, has left its mark on the landscape and continues to reverberate. This is understandably focused on the emotive human aspects with less emphasis on the vast, on-going building programme undertaken by the estate. This included new roads and bridges, laying out of new crofting settlements to receive those evicted, the development of salmon and sea fisheries with their appropriate processing stations, the building of churches, manses, schools and inns, the expansion of farms with new farmhouses and steadings all providing employment.

Three generations of estate surveyors have left their mark on this building activity. George Alexander, a Golspie builder/architect, produced neat manses and improved farmhouses, the elevations and plans published by James Loch (see p.58) in *An Account of the Improvements on the Estate of Lord Stafford* (1820). More sophisticated was his successor, Alexander Coupar, Estate Superintendent of Works, whose principal undertaking was the restoration and remodelling of Dornoch Cathedral in 1835. Thirdly, in 1857, William Fowler was appointed Estate Surveyor: he designed many estate cottages, shooting lodges and schools, much of his work reflecting the

influence of the London architect, George Devey (1820-86) who designed buildings on the estate from the late 1850s (executed by Fowler) initiating an unmistakable Sutherland estate pattern. Cottages and houses have steep, sloping roofs and deep eaves, neat dormers are often fitted with sliding sash windows found nowhere else in the north, bold chimney-stacks are set diagonally on rectangular bases, terminating with simple, stalwart freestone copes, or rise as tall rubble stalks from the wallhead. The masonry is usually rugged rubble, some railway stations and shooting lodges sport timber arcaded verandas while characteristic vernacular gable-end skewputts (brackets), sometimes dated, support plain bargeboards, stamping buildings with a traditional feature. For schools, the estate style continued in Sutherland even after the 1872 Education Act, when they were financed by public funds rather than by the landowner.

Rogart, 1864; characteristic mid-19th-century Sutherland estate house probably designed by William Fowler: note rubble masonry, tall chimney-stacks, plain bargeboards supported on projecting stone brackets and dormer window. Large S under ducal coronet in gable apex

Manses, inns and farmhouses constructed between 1803 and 1833 are normally adorned with the joint arms of the Marquis of Stafford and Countess of Sutherland; after elevation in 1833 to the Dukedom of Sutherland, the usual insignia is a large S set in a plaque, occasionally dignified by a ducal coronet.

As elsewhere in the Highlands, the improvement of roads was an important undertaking. Between 1803-20 the Commission for Highland Roads & Bridges, with Thomas Telford as chief engineer, constructed roads northwards. The opening up of the Highlands by road (and later by rail) facilitated communication and trade, in particular the droving of cattle south to the annual cattle fairs. Further road building was undertaken by the Sutherland estate, between 1816 and 1831 from Bonar Bridge to Lochinver and in the 1830s north and west from Bighouse to Loch Assynt. Inns were constructed to provide shelter and refreshment for travellers.

Stafford / Sutherland armorial, 1808, Sutherland Arms, Golspie

Road and bridge building have continued; fine 20th-century bridges with spare, elegant profiles span former ferry crossings.

As might be expected from a family enriched by English railways, the House of Sutherland encouraged the establishment of a rail link north of Inverness. The section of the Highland Railway from Golspie to Helmsdale (Sutherland Railway) was entirely the responsibility of the 3rd Duke in 1868-71. The station buildings are designed in the well-

Crask Inn and Bridge, c.1815, between Altnaharra and Tongue; one of many inns built to provide shelter for travellers

Top Dunstalking, Kinbrace; corrugated-iron cottage, the materials probably transported from Glasgow by train. Above Speirs & Co, Glasgow; advertisement for prefabricated buildings Northern Times, c.18 Oct 1906. Right Hope Lodge, gabled, slate-hung shooting lodge with timber-arcaded veranda, c.1875, designed by William Fowler for Sutherland estate

Sutherland estate cottage. Note characteristic gable-end skewputts supporting plain bargeboards and dated 1885

established estate style.

The coming of the railway opened up opportunities for firms such as Speirs & Co, Glasgow, makers of prefabricated corrugated-iron buildings. Churches, halls, cottages, bakers' shops and even a hospital were transported north in sections, carried onwards from the nearest railhead in carts drawn by doughty horses, driven by even doughtier carters. Their brightly painted exteriors cheer glen and village alike.

The many substantial 19th-century shooting lodges sited in distant glens and at loch sides throughout Sutherland became an investment in a form of tourism, let to sportsmen attended by hardy local keepers and ghillies. The rents and fees enriched, and continue to support, these lodges and their employees.

Single-storey cottages, often with later roof dormers, and one-and-half-storey houses with gabled dormers, form the traditional housing of the countryside. The latter date from the 1890s and later, after the Crofters' Act of 1886 provided security of land tenure, enabling crofters to achieve a relative prosperity during the years before 1914.

The ecclesiastical and secular history of Sutherland is clearly mirrored in her buildings and architecture, which includes brochs, an ancient cathedral and small parish churches, castles and cottages, lairds' houses and shooting lodges, farms and crofts, lighthouses, harbours and hydro-electric power stations. The settlement pattern of the medieval kirkton, the fishing village and the linear development of the 19th-century crofting township reveal and record social change and development. These buildings, rather than ancient archaeology, are the subject of this guide.

Organisation of the Guide

The guide follows a route from south-east Sutherland and the Dornoch Firth, northwards to the shores of the Pentland Firth and then to the north-west coast, illustrating and interpreting the landscape and history of the specific places through the buildings and architecture. Starting at Kincardine and Ardgay it proceeds to Strathcarron, Croick and Carbisdale. From Bonar Bridge and Invershin westwards to Strath Oykel; eastwards from Bonar Bridge to Spinningdale, Skibo and Clashmore; then Lairg, Altnaharra and Rogart followed by Dornoch. Embo, The Mound, Golspie, Brora and Helmsdale follow the east coast northwards in geographical progression. From Helmsdale the guide continues up the Strath of Kildonan to Kinbrace, Forsinard and Strath Halladale to Bighouse on the north coast. The route hugs the Pentland Firth coastline to Bettyhill with a diversion to Strathnaver; then to Tongue, Eriboll, Durness and Cape Wrath from whence the guide follows the west coast taking in Kinlochbervie, Achfary, Stoer and Lochinver, finishing at Inchnadamph, Ledmore and Elphin.

Text Arrangement

Entries for principal buildings follow the sequence of name (or number), address, date and architect (if known). Lesser buildings are sometimes contained within the same paragraphs. Text in the smaller columns is illustrative or anecdotal of the social, cultural or historic background to the buildings and architecture of Sutherland.

Maps

Principal locations are named on the district map: there are also street maps for Dornoch, Golspie and Helmsdale. The reference numbers relate to the numbers in the text and not to page numbers. The maps have been prepared by Calum McKenzie, by courtesy of the Law & Dunbar-Nasmith Partnership.

Access

Where buildings described in this guide are open to the public this is clearly stated at the end of the entry. When churches are locked, permission to view can usually be obtained, the church notice board being often helpful. Most mansions, houses and shooting lodges are private and approached by private roads: some can be seen from the public highway. Readers are asked to respect the occupiers' privacy.

Sponsors

Publication to allow for a reasonably priced guide has been made possible through the support of The Manifold Trust, Caithness & Sutherland Enterprise, Highland Regional Council, Sutherland District Council, The Countess of Sutherland, Cupa Slates, Society of Northern Architects and The Landmark Trust. All photographs credited to Historic Scotland have been donated by that agency.

Above 'The modern and old house of the tenants of the Reay Country'. New Statistical Account, 1840. Smoke from a central hearth seeped through the thatch of the earlier vernacular cottages, which was removed to manure the ground. These thatched cottages lingered on in north-west Sutherland well into the age of photography, see Stoer, p.101. Below Dunrobin Castle roofscape. Bottom Sutherland-style numerals found on later 19th-century datestones. Note attenuated 'tail' to nine and six

9

Beaton

Dornoch Firth Bridge, 1991

Kincardine Parish, on the southern banks of the Kyle of Sutherland and the Dornoch Firth and embracing parts of Strath Oykel, was ceded to Sutherland District in the local-government reorganisation of 1974. It is, however, essentially part of Ross & Cromarty with which it has historic ties, particularly in Strathcarron which runs many miles westwards and where many of the landowners belonged to Ross-shire. The hills fall to the southern shores of the Dornoch Firth, a deep inlet flanked by hills, the shores formerly punctuated with regular ferry sites. North and west of Bonar Bridge the firth becomes the Kyle of Sutherland, fed by the triple waters of the rivers Carron, Oykel and Shin.

James Boag (or **Boog**) was a Lowland carpenter who established himself in Sutherland, first at Golspie Tower and then at Dornoch. He was a rough man, who *terrified all the schoolboys, as well as every inmate of his own house, by the violence of his temper and his readiness to take offence*. His buildings were mostly in the simplest style of 18th-century Scottish vernacular.

Old Kincardine Parish Church, 1799, probably James Boag
Traditional late 18th-century Highland kirk; simple, low, harled rectangle, one door lintel inscribed MAG 1799 for Master Andrew Gallie, Minister, 1780-1803. He graduated Master of Arts, King's College, Aberdeen, and was, therefore, entitled to call himself Master. Burial ground with Pictish stone enclosed by drystone wall constructed in 1838. **Kincardine House**, 1769, plain former parish manse with later projecting drawing-room wing added in 1827.

The village of **Ardgay** developed after the bridging of the Kyle of Sutherland at Bonar Bridge, 1812, and the arrival of the railway. Railway **station**, *c*.1865, Murdoch Paterson for Joseph Mitchell & Co, railway engineers; gabled front and platform canopy supported by slender cast-iron columns together with cast-iron footbridge, resembling others on this stretch of line. As soon as post arrived by train, Ardgay became the local postal centre. The plain **post office**, 1909, A Maitland & Sons, retains the sorting office with all original fittings which include desks equipped with *pigeon holes* and swivel stools, besides the post office with contemporary counter. There can be few other such post-office interiors surviving in Scotland.

Above *Ardgay Post Office.*
Left *Sorting office: remarkable survival of post-office fittings.*
Below *Icehouse, Ardgay*

Clach Eiteag boulder, an irregular white quartzite rock, mounted in the centre of the village, commemorates an annual three-day fair or market. Substantial early 19th-century **icehouse** built into slope for insulation.

STRATHCARRON
Strathcarron runs westward to **Croick** and **Glen Calvie**, an expansive strath scattered with farms, crofts and shooting lodges.

Kincardine Free Church:
Below *Plaster decoration on pulpit sounding board.* Left *Tall windows light the interior, flanking projecting minister's porch*

Kincardine Free Church, Lower Gledfield, dated 1849
Tall, imposing, grey rubble rectangular building with minister's porch projecting

This bell captured in a French ship of War of 74 guns was gifted by Sir John Ross of Balnagoun (sic) Bart in the year of 1778 to the Parish of Kincardine.

When Britain's Navies did a World Control
And Spread her Empire to the farthest Pole;
High stood our Hero in the Rolls of Fame,
And LOCKHART, then became a Deathliss name.
This Bell no more shall witness Blood or Gore,
Nor shall his Voice mix with Cannon's roar
But to Kincardine by the Hero given Shall call the Sinner to the Peace of Heaven.

Inscription below bell removed from Kincardine Church to hang above door at Ardgay Church of Scotland.

Gledfield House: Below Late 18th-century doorpiece. Bottom Late 18th-century central block with extensive Edwardian additions

Beaton

from centre of south elevation, flanked each side by two long round-headed windows. Urn finial and bellcote at east and west gable apices respectively. The austere five-sided galleried interior is dominated by a handsome three-decker pulpit crowned with domed sounding board with fine plaster decoration. The associated **Free Church school and schoolhouse**, 1852, A Maitland, is a pleasant single-storeyed range now two dwellings.

Ardgay Church of Scotland (former UF Church), Lower Gledfield, 1908, A Maitland & Sons, has windows enlivened with simple Gothic cusping. *The large and well-toned bell,* previously in Old Kincardine Parish Church, hangs above the door.

Carron Bridge, 1818, Alex Wilson (engineer) Single graceful arch flanked on one side by a small pedestrian arch. Worn inscription states: *This bridge was erected by the 2nd District of Roads in Rofsshire in MDCCCXVIII Alex and Thos Muirson Architects,* with second, roughly scratched inscription *192(?) by Alex Grant Architect* presumably recording 20th-century repairs.

Gledfield House, 1895-1907, Ross & Macbeth Simple *gentleman's residence* of *c*.1800 transformed into a pink-harled rambling mansion, with wide bowed bays, shaped gables, generous use of ashlar margins and additional wings containing drawing room and ballroom. Notable Edwardian plaster ceilings in 18th-century style. Large **walled garden** with Ionic-columned **pavilion**; **stable range**,

Beaton

_c._1900, with ridge bellcote and applied timber-frame decoration: substantial **mill**, disused since 1950. At Dounie, the remains of **An Dun broch** are sited by the river.

Gruinards Lodge, 1896-7, A Maitland & Sons Baronial gabled shooting lodge constructed of bull-faced rubble with some mock timber-framing detailing. Entrance porch in base of four-stage tower with projecting stair turret and corbelled and crenellated upper stage. Gruinards (Greenyards) was _cleared_ of its inhabitants as late as 1854 in the cause of agricultural _improvement_ particularly the creation of large fields, a brutal event known as the _Massacre of the Rosses_ (colour page 49).

Andrew Maitland (1802-94), a native of Keith, Banffshire, who trained in Edinburgh, was probably an assistant to William Robertson, Elgin (1786-1841), settling in Tain in 1842 after supervising work for Robertson in the Black Isle. He established a successful business despite near-bankruptcy as a shareholder in the City of Glasgow Bank, liquidated in 1882. The firm became A Maitland & Sons from 1873 after James and Andrew Maitland joined their father.

Beaton

Gruinards Lodge

Braelangwell, from 1748
An attractive, rambling shooting lodge incorporating building periods from the mid-18th century onwards. These include a house, _c._1800, with radial fanlight and a single-storey wing with pretty lattice glazing. Set amongst fine trees, Braelangwell is of historic interest, long the property of the Rosses of Balnagown, Easter Ross (see _Ross & Cromarty_ in this series). There is a Ross datestone of 1748; in 1840 the house was described as _the picturesque summer residence of Sir Charles Ross of Balnagown_.

Amat Lodge, core, _c._1800, later alterations
Tall, many-windowed house with crenellated wallhead from which rises a square tower, the roof punctuated by 20th-century dormers. Amat stands near the junction of Glen Calvie and Strath Cuileannach, the site, in 1790, of a _preaching station_ for local inhabitants for whom Kincardine Parish Church was too far away for worship. This was succeeded by Croick Church of Scotland in 1827 while the small, plain Free Church was constructed near East Amat, _c._1880 (now converted as a

Amat Lodge

Beaton

Above *Croick Church*. Right *Old manse*

dwelling-house). **Glencalvie Lodge**, 1892, A Maitland & Sons, pink-washed and gabled with angle turrets linked by a veranda dignifying the front elevation.

Croick Church, 1827, Thomas Telford Standard Parliamentary T-plan design (see p.4), white-harled with ashlar margins. Low building with no provision for galleries. Unusually complete interior with pulpit fitted with iron bracket to hold the baptismal font and fronted by the Precentor's desk; there are box pews for elders and a long central communion table. Original lattice-pane glazing, some with graffiti incised by crofters evicted from Glencalvie in 1845 and 1854. *The church is usually open and in occasional use* (colour page 49).

Outside Croick Church **burial ground** the remains of a **broch** (see p.57) are scattered on a mound between church and river. The former **manse**, also 1827, Thomas Telford, was built to the single-storey, H-plan Parliamentary manse design (see p.4): now a holiday home.

INVERCHARRON & CARBISDALE
Invercharron House, *c*.1700 onwards Two-storey, white-harled rambling house with crowstepped gables, pedimented dormers and advanced bowed bays. The house has grown comfortably for 200 years from the mid-18th century onwards, accruing a homely grace and dignity. **Culrain Mains**, 1821, wright Nicholas Vass, Tain; mason, John Rose, Cromarty; regular-fronted, two-storey, three-bay house with painted margins. Just to the west of Culrain is the site of the Battle of Carbisdale, 1650, in which James Graham, Marquis of Montrose, was defeated. A marked walk of the battle ground starts from Culrain.

Left *Carbisdale Castle.* Below
Elegant marble chimney-piece,
Carbisdale Castle

1 **Carbisdale Castle**, 1910-11, W S Weatherley
& F E Jones
Dramatically crowning a wooded spur
overlooking a magnificent panorama of valley,
sea and hills. This was the site of the earlier
Culrain Lodge, greatly extended in English
Tudor into a soaring L-plan pile with square
crenellated clock tower rising above the gabled
roofline. An octagonal turret punctuates the re-
entrant angle while the main entrance is
fronted by a somewhat incongruous pilastered
porte-cochère. Dark rubble masonry contrasts
with the many-mullioned and transomed
windows faced in pale sandstone. Castle
surrounded by crenellated wall, the entrance
flanked by imposing circular piers with fine
gates. Even in the building's present role as a
youth hostel, the interior remains grand.
Marble statuary graces the entrance hall,
furnished with a beautiful carved white marble
chimney-piece, one of many still *in situ.* There
is an imposing staircase and amongst other
original fittings are the bookcases adorning the
former library.

Carbisdale Castle was built by
Duchess Blair (Mary C Blair) second
wife of the 3rd Duke of Sutherland
but unpopular with his family. He
died in 1892, leaving his widow a
personal fortune: she is said to have
been refused land in Sutherland by
his heir so built her castle just
inside Ross-shire yet overlooking
Sutherland.

BONAR BRIDGE & MIGDALE

Bonar Bridge village grew at the Bonar Ferry,
where Thomas Telford found the best site for a
bridge over the Kyle of Sutherland in 1812,
easing the way of drovers and their cattle from
north to south by eliminating the need to swim
stock over the dangerous and fast-flowing water.

Bonar Bridge beside the Kyle of
Sutherland with salmon fishing in
foreground

The village is strung out along the banks of the Kyle of Sutherland, the confluence of the rich salmon rivers, Shin, Oykel and Carron. Many of the houses in Bonar Bridge are the simple two-storey, three-window dwellings that formed the nucleus of the first settlement close to the bridge.

Bonar Bridge, 1973, A A Cullen Wallace (engineer) with Crouch & Hogg
Elegant bowstring bridge of deceptive simplicity executed in grey metal, worthy successor to Thomas Telford's graceful arch of 1812, followed in 1892-3 by Crouch & Hogg's three-arch, mild-steel viaduct, demolished 1971.

Bonar Bridge, Thomas Telford, 1812, aquatint by Wm Daniell, 1821

Bonar Bridge, 1892-3

Bonar Bridge, 1973

Bank of Scotland, 1865, Alexander Ross
Handsome former Caledonian Bank, with symmetrical three-window elevations front and rear; designed to impress both from the road at

the front and the river at the rear. Harled with much decorative use of ashlar margins and cornices.

Migdale Hospital, 1863-5, Andrew Maitland
Former Sutherland Combination Poorhouse, opened 6 Nov 1865, built to serve a combination of all parochial boards, hence the name. Long, dignified white-harled two-storey gabled range fronted by single-storey staff quarters. The design may have been standard; similar former poorhouse at Chanonry, 1859, by William Lawrie (see *Ross & Cromarty* in this series); others in Nairn and Inverness.

Church of Scotland, 1911-13,
James Maitland of A Maitland & Sons
Gothic, chunky rubble with contrasting dressings framing lancet windows. Square tower with short spire. Cast-iron aisle arcade columns and collar-beam roof with decorated brackets. Generous stained glass, the window behind pulpit depicting local fishing and farming activities. This church, largely paid for by Andrew Carnegie of Skibo, replaced the former parish church sited in the **burial ground** east of the village near the prominent site of **Dun Creich fort** and a ferry crossing to Fearn.

Migdale Free Church, 1881,
A Maitland & Sons
Replacing that of 1843. Buttressed gabled frontage with recessed centre entrance flanked by narrow lights; long triple lancets and apex bellcote. Interior dominated by high two-decker pulpit with sounding board and flanked each side by balustraded stairs. Cusped panelled gallery supported by cast-iron columns with Corinthian capitals; brass lamp brackets. Plain **manse**, 1849, and former **school**, 1846, now church room, with *Search the Scriptures* inscribed on lintel. An interesting group, indicative of the efforts and strength of the Free Church movement in the Highlands.

Top *Bank of Scotland.* Middle *Migdale Hospital.* Above *Church of Scotland*

Balblair House, *c.*1830-40
Pretty villa on hillside overlooking the Kyle of Sutherland. Deep-eaved symmetrical harled frontage enlivened with sandstone margins but marred by an enlarged window. Entrance flanked by mirrored **gate lodges**, each with bowed front to driveway and tall coped chimney-stacks.

Above *Shin railway viaduct and Carbisdale Castle.* Below *Invershin Farm, former salmon station*

Salmon were a historic source of wealth, caught mainly in the rivers of north and north-east Scotland in both nets and cruives (traps). Until *c.*1800 they were salted and exported in barrels after which they were parboiled in a pickle and packed in ice. The boiling houses, with their large hearths, wallhead chimney-stacks and icehouses are a feature of the salmon stations. Ice was collected from rivers or specially constructed shallow ponds and stored in semi-subterranean stone vaults; if compressed and drained, it would keep up to a year. Packed in ice, the fish were then exported by sea.

[John] Mitchell, father of the more famous civil engineer Joseph, . . . produced a . . . design for a three-arch bridge [at Invershin]. *His plan was checked and modified by* [Thomas] *Telford who strongly recommended to the trustees both the design and Mitchell, on account of his* 'experience, talents and integrity' . . . *The contract specified . . .* 'neat well-dressed Rubble masonry' *of local stone and . . . a* 'coping of Free stone to be neatly Chizzel-drafted on the parapets', *which along with the lower course, was to be of stone from the Tain quarries.*
Malcolm Bangor-Jones, 'The Making of the Road to Lochinver', *The Northern Times*, 30 March 1990

Shin railway viaduct, 1867, Joseph Mitchell & Murdoch Paterson
An imposing 70m (230ft) iron-truss bridge with semicircular arched approaches, constructed for the Sutherland Railway.

² **INVERSHIN**
Invershin Farm, *c.*1800-20
Former salmon fishing station and manager's house. Courtyard complex includes two vaulted icehouses, boiling house with tall chimney-stack and stores, weathervane sporting salmon silhouette and regularly fronted house. One of the icehouses is still insulated by its traditional turf roof. A short track links complex to river frontage, sheltered by the mound of Invershin Castle (no building survives) at the confluence of the Oykel and Shin rivers.

Old Shin Bridge, 1822, John Mitchell
Fine, high three-arch rubble bridge spanning River Shin (now bypassed) (colour page 49).

Shin Power Station, 1958, Shearer & Annand (architects); Sir W Halcrow (engineer) Tall, rectangular, red rubble range clasped at base by low single-storey ranges. The deep-eaved power station slots neatly into Sutherland building traditions. Here, as elsewhere, Scottish Hydro-Electric has built in natural stone and sited its power station sympathetically into the landscape.

ACHANY GLEN

The **River Shin** flows through wooded Achany Glen. From the viewing platform at the **Shin Falls**, the salmon can be seen swimming in the swirling pool below the waterfall, preparing to leap upwards through the spray on their way up-river to their spawning grounds.

Achany House, from *c*.1810
Dignified three-storey symmetrically fronted house of at least three builds overlooking the Shin gorge. Originally a two-storey, three-bay house, widened with outer bowed bays, *c*.1845; later pedimented dormers, 1885, probably A Maitland & Sons, together with rear addition. The front windows in the centre, original portion, have beaded panelled shutters, a house carpentry pattern which found favour in the north roughly between 1810-30.

3 **Aultnagar Lodge Hotel**, 1910-11, R J Macbeth
Mock black-and-white timber-framed upper floors to wide gabled, many windowed house; an incongruous but effective *English* style for its Highland location. Built by Andrew Carnegie as a retreat from the social whirl of Skibo Castle. Nearby **Achinduich**, from 1800, a plain but dignified house with margined windows; once centre of a large sheep farm.

Achany House: Below *Centre block c.1810, mid-19th-century outer wings: sketch from early photograph.* Bottom *Conical drum-tower roofs and pedimented dormers added 1885*

Robert J Macbeth (1857-1912) trained with Hugh Mackenzie, architect, Elgin, and joined Alexander Ross, Inverness, in 1880, becoming a partner in 1887. In 1907 he set up on his own in Inverness, subsequently with an office in Forres. He practised widely in the Highlands, his later secular buildings with a chunky Free Style flavour and a nod to Gothic. Though Skibo Castle was redesigned by Alexander Ross, Macbeth was involved and, after 1907, worked independently for Andrew Carnegie. He designed many churches and manses for the United Free Church between 1906-10.

Aultnagar Lodge Hotel: Left *With polygonal sun parlour (right).* Below *Inglenook*

STRATH OYKEL, ROSEHALL & GLEN CASSLEY

Strath Oykel is a broad valley with farms on the better arable land, crofts on the less fertile slopes, bounded by forestry and rounded moorland hills. The **Bonar Bridge/Ledmore/ Lochinver road** (A837) was constructed between 1821-7 by local trustees, the work supervised by John Mitchell, Thomas Telford's trusty assistant. It winds its often lonely but always scenicly beautiful way westwards to the Assynt. The valley widens at Rosehall at the confluence of the Rivers Cassley and Oykel.

Rosehall Church of Scotland (former UF Church), *c*.1908; associated former manse, 1909, R J Macbeth. **Free Church**, *c*.1844 and now disused, has an unusual hexagonal minister's porch. These two churches are but a couple of hundred yards apart, an apposite example of church building by the United Free congregations between 1906-10 after their schism with the Free Church. Both are simple rubble buildings erected to serve scattered congregations.

Rosehall Bridge, 1825, fine twin-arched bridge spanning the River Cassley. Gabled **Glen Rossal Lodge**, 1871, Alexander Ross, sited on the hillside amidst birch woods, the associated **kennels** by the roadside.
Glencassley Castle, *c*.1860 and 1875, also Alexander Ross. Grandiose shooting lodge embellished by a square tower overlooking broad Glen Cassley.

Rosehall House, 1818-25 (dated 1822), style of William Robertson
Wide, grey stone gabled mansion, the austere

Below Rosehall Bridge over River Cassley. Bottom Glencassley Castle. Bottom right Rosehall House

Historic Scotland

Historic Scotland

Beaton

Richard Dunning, 2nd Lord Ashburton (Devon, from where he originated), had connections with Sutherland through his wife, Anne Cuninghame. He bought Rosehall estate in 1806, developing it until his death in 1823: he linked Rosehall with the River Oykel by canal and built mill and church besides other buildings, some of which he designed himself. When Rosehall House burnt down in May 1817, destroying his well-stocked library, Ashburton immediately set about rebuilding.

open pedimented frontage relieved by contrasting tooled warm brown Moray sandstone dressings, large windows, deep eaves and slightly set-back outer bays. Wide pilastered and corniced doorpiece. The stone from Moray was shipped up-river and then by a short canal to the house site; all that remains of the canal is now the Rosehall duckpond. The house stands in parkland, has a walled garden, estate cottages and three lodges fronting the main road. Also **The Cone House**; probably the mid-18th-century estate barn or girnal in which rents-in-kind were stored, later used to season fir cones for afforestation. Steeply crowstepped original west gable. Converted and extended as dwelling-house, 1932, Horne & Murray, with further addition in 1967, R I Beaton. **The Barracks** (near War Memorial) are early 19th-century cottages which housed masons and carpenters working on Rosehall House.

Brae Doune footbridge

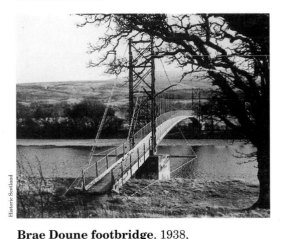

Historic Scotland

Brae Doune footbridge, 1938, John M Henderson & Co (engineers) Sixty-metre (200ft) long, graceful suspension bridge borne on steel-girder pylons. The 20th-century footbridge eases passage at this long-established river crossing (colour page 49). Small walled **burial ground** on hillside above the bridge; one of the earliest tombstones is to Hugh Ross, who died in 1828, and his wife Grace: he was a Royal Marine for 30 years, serving far from home. **Old Oykel Bridge**, 1825, single masonry span now bypassed. **Oykel Bridge Hotel**, 1831, and later: originally an inn associated with the road completed by 1831 and intended to shelter and refresh travellers on the east/west journey. The hotel is now popular with fishermen.

George Davidson and John Findlay, masons from Rothes in Morayshire, were given the job of building all the bridges [between Bonar Bridge and Lochinver]. *With the addition of a bridge over the Culag at Lochinver (see p.104) they were to build 20 bridges. Eight bridges, including the fine two-arch bridge over the Cassley at Rosehall costing £827 and the bridge over the Oykel costing £330, were completed in 1825. All were judged to have been well built . . .*
Malcolm Bangor-Jones, 'The Making of the Road to Lochinver', *The Northern Times*, 30 March 1990

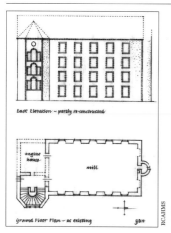

East Elevation – partly re-constructed

engine house / mill

ground Floor Plan – as existing

Above *Spinningdale cotton mill, reconstruction.* Right *Spinningdale mill, constructed in 1792-3 to bring industry to the Highlands*

Spinningdale cotton mill was established in 1792-3 by the combined efforts of local landowners and others, notably George Dempster of Dunnichen and Skibo, and David Dale of Lanark, to form the Balnoe Company. Dempster was a man of great humanity and sought to provide work and land for the destitute in his Highland parish, offering land at a nominal rent to those prepared to improve it. The short-lived cotton-spinning venture was intended to provide employment locally, but was never revived after the fire of 1806. Though seemingly isolated, the cove below the mill offered shelter where *vessels of 50 tons burden can land their cargoes*, a reminder of the primacy of marine transport.

Ospisdale House

SPINNINGDALE, SKIBO & CLASHMORE

Eastwards from Bonar Bridge the road follows the north coast of the Dornoch Firth, past the burial ground, once the site of Creich Parish Church. Scattered crofts are on land *lotted* by kindly landlords in the late 19th century to those evicted from elsewhere, of which **Feorlig**, Spinningdale, is a good example, the former thatch replaced by a cheerful red-painted corrugated-iron roof.

Spinningdale cotton mill, 1792-3, James Boag
Ruinous but impressive monument to philanthropic industrialism. Three-storey range with full-height canted stair-tower lit by Venetian windows in the front elevation and semicircular latrine tower at north gable. This spinning-jenny factory was damaged by fire in 1806 and never rebuilt. A dangerous ruin but fully visible from the road.

Ospisdale House, from 18th century
Gracious house set in fields overlooking the Dornoch Firth. Originally a three-window front, sympathetically widened by an additional bay in the 1930s. Columned portico, shallow bowed outer bays enhanced by giant panelled pilasters, crenellated wallhead. Substantial **farm steading**, dated 1827 and 1845, datestone initialed DG for Dougal Gilchrist whose family owned the property from 1783 until the 20th century. The site, however, is old. There was a tower house at Ospisdale by 1568: an estate map of 1705 reveals a small house.

Skibo Castle, dated 1900, Ross & Macbeth
Incorporating a large baronial house of 1880 by

Clarke & Bell, Glasgow. The site is earlier for there was a castle here belonging to the Bishops of Caithness and Sutherland until 1565. Extraordinary castellated edifice, three and four storeys high, displaying every baronial revival detail in the book! Drum towers, battlements, bartizans, caphouses, corbelling, all are at Skibo in impressive profusion. The interior is equally richly fitted, in heavy late-Victorian fashion.

Terraced gardens descending from the castle were laid out in 1904 by Thomas Mawson. There is a **swimming pool** of *c.*1900 housed in a large glazed hall, with a flue passing underground a few hundred yards to terminate within one of the castle towers. The swimming pool could be converted as a ballroom by the simple expedient of covering the pool with a dance floor. Other estate buildings include a former **'electric house'** and private **telephone exchange**, **glass houses** with decorative thistle finials and cast-iron brattishing (ridge crest) besides a model **farm steading** with pretty **dairy**, its roof swept over a rustic veranda.

West Lodge, 1907, R J Macbeth, crenellated gate lodge with tower; heavily rock-faced circular gatepiers flanking fine iron gates.

Newton Point, small late 18th-century rubble shore-side warehouse for the storage of processed flax, imported to be spun locally.

Carnegie Hall, Clashmore, 1907, style of R J Macbeth
Strong, chunky Arts & Crafts village hall with battered tooled ashlar basecourse, angle buttresses and mock timber-studding detail; gabled porch, squat ridge ventilator and turn-of-the-century glass. Plain interior with some original furnishings.

Top left *Skibo Castle, west elevation; earlier house at left.* Top *Skibo Castle.* Above *Skibo Castle, dining-room chimney-piece*

Skibo Castle was the residence of the Bishop of Caithness, whose see was established at Dornoch from 1224. After 1565 it passed through many owners: finally purchased in 1895 by Andrew Carnegie, the Scottish/American steel magnate and philanthropist, becoming his cherished Highland home. Carnegie's architect was Alexander Ross. Carnegie hung a portrait of Ross at Skibo Castle inscribed *Our architect yet our friend.*

Alexander Ross (1834-1925) inherited his father's Inverness practice in 1853 aged 19. *Not surprisingly, business was a little slack . . . From 1865 until the end of the century and beyond Ross was firmly established . . . He was the colossus among Highland architects . . . in Ross are drawn together the threads of 19th-century Highland architecture, eclectic, practical and at times touching on genius, at others of the drabbest, but always stamped with a force of personality.* John Gifford, Scottish Georgian Society (AHSS) *Bulletin*, 1980

CYDERHALL

*An unusual Norse (place-name) . . . is **Cyder Hall**, which has early forms in* Sywardhoth *1230,* Sytheraw *1275 and* Siddera *1654. This is reputed to be the burial place of Earl Sigurd who, according to the saga* (Orkneyinga Saga) *account, died from blood poisoning when he was scratched by the bucktooth of Maelbrigit, Mormaer of Moray. Sigurd, having slain Maelbrigit in battle, was imprudently carrying his adversary's head home to Caithness on his saddlebow, when the fatal scratch was acquired. It is certainly the most colourful of the Norse names in the area, and one of the few which can be said to be truly commemorative.*
Ian A Fraser, in *The Firthlands of Ross and Sutherland*, 1986

Meikle Ferry slipway, early 19th-century ramped pier, formerly linking Dornoch with Tain (see *Ross & Cromarty* in this series) across the narrows of the Dornoch Firth. Before the bridging of the Kyle of Sutherland at Bonar in 1812 this was the principal link with Ross-shire and the south, as it has become again with the construction of the **Dornoch Firth Bridge**, 1991, Crouch, Hogg and Waterman with Ove Arup, spanning the firth just east of Meikle Ferry.

Cyderhall Farm, 1818

Superior regularly fronted farmhouse; with its model farm steading, this was one of the *improved* buildings on the Sutherlands' estate, the house probably succeeding that noted by Pennant in 1769. Sigurd the Mighty, 1st Earl of Orkney, is reputed to have been buried close by at Sigurd's Howe on Cnoc Skardie, *c.* AD 982. In the mid-13th century glass for Dornoch Cathedral was made at *Sidderay*.

Loch Shin and Lairg

LAIRG

Lairg spreads out at the southern end of Loch Shin, once a ferry crossing over the fast-flowing River Shin and sited at the junction of roads from all four points of the compass in Sutherland. Its immediate hinterland is scattered with crofts, farms and shooting lodges. As the only substantial village in central Sutherland, it exists to serve a far-flung rural population, besides offering facilities to passing tourists. The active GPO sorting office receives and delivers post many miles to distant western and northern settlements, including the Pentland Firth coast. The annual sheep sale is the largest in Scotland, the sale ground and stock pens close by the railway station.

The buildings are varied, mostly unexceptional, clustered by the lochside and spilling down the hillside behind the village. A bit bleak in winter, but in summer sunshine sparkling with reflected light from the expansive waters of Loch Shin.

Sutherland Arms, dated 1864, incorporates earlier and later work; a typical gabled Sutherland estate building of the 1860s with chimney-stacks set diamondwise on rectangular bases and deep eaves. **Tourist Information Office**, dated 1844, is probably former gighouse and stable to an earlier hotel and a small **icehouse** built into the slope near the main entrance is now a fuel store. In contrast, in the High Street there is a somewhat incongruous 1930s white-harled, two-storey, flat-roofed range with shops in the ground floor. **Church of Scotland**, 1845-6, William Leslie; buttressed plain grey granite on knoll overlooking village with commanding views over Loch Shin. The gabled **manse** is said to date from 1846.

Church of Scotland manse

Scottish Hydro-Electric dam & power station, 1958, Shearer & Annand (architects), power station; Sir M Macdonald (consulting engineer)
Impressive concrete dam and stalwartly massed square rubble power station, an angle drum tower adding Scottish flavour to the design.

Free Church, from 1845, with later alterations
Forms a closely knit group consisting of church, **manse** and **former school**, the church lit by pointed-headed lancets.

Scottish Hydro-Electric dam & power station

Burial ground (site of old church) crowns the hill above Lairg, enjoying a panoramic outlook. Grandiose **memorial** to Sir James Matheson (1796-1878), a Corinthian-columned domed marble three-bay loggia below which stands a square marble pedestal (A Veigl, Menton, France) with medallion (J E Boehm) depicting Sir James. The capitals are decorated with carved opium poppy heads, recording the commodity on which the Jardine Matheson Far East trading empire was founded. The cosmopolitan sophistication of this monument is the quintessence of architectural surprise in the Highlands (colour page 49). Also in the burial ground is a simple **memorial** to William Mackay whose *Narrative of the Shipwreck of the Juno* (1795) is embodied in Byron's *Don Juan*.

Matheson memorial

Murray Memorial, 1877
A simple obelisk near Shinness, now somewhat masked by forestry (a roadside sign points the

Top *'The Duke's toothpick': large plough hauled by steam engine at work at Coaboll, near Lairg, 1873-6.* Above *West Shinness Lodge*

Beaton

Rogart, decorative cast-iron gate and railings, probably brought by rail

Beaton

Northern Times

way to the site), which commemorates another pioneer, Kenneth Murray of Geanies, Easter Ross, who, on behalf of the Duke of Sutherland, broke up great tracts of land at Gruids, Colaboll and Tirryside with a *huge steam plough* nicknamed *the Duke's toothpick*, between 1873-6. This work excited considerable interest in farming circles and was visited by the Prince of Wales. **West Shinness Lodge**, mid/late 18th century, has grown sympathetically to become a plain L-plan house. This was the birthplace of Sir James Matheson.

Sallachy is a large, gaunt shooting lodge prominent on the south bank of Loch Shin. Near by **Sallachy Broch** has upstanding turf-covered walls and is clearly visible.

The A838 travels north-west the length of Loch Shin and Loch More to Laxford Bridge. North from Lairg the A836 passes through the emptiness of central Sutherland, the *Flow Country*, with its vast expanse of moorland, streams and rivers, lochs and lochans, isolated shooting lodges and a few farms and crofts, whose inhabitants travel long distances on rough tracks for schools and services. Central Sutherland is probably the largest least-populated area in Great Britain. The road to Tongue via Altnaharra, with its many single-span bridges, was constructed under the supervision of Thomas Telford with the Commission for Highland Roads & Bridges and completed in 1819.

ALTNAHARRA

A small village in the centre of Sutherland at the head of Loch Naver.

Altnaharra Hotel, 1877, reconstructed after fire, 1956, R I Beaton
Gabled, crowstepped and white harled with inner courtyard; original bowed porch

complemented, in 1956, by full-height bowed bay window and buttresses. **Primary School** and **Schoolhouse**, 1962, also by Beaton, is a low whitewashed range hugging the sloping site, quite at home in its setting. **Church of Scotland** (former Free Church), 1854-5, Hugh Mackay, plain rubble building with later Celtic cross prominent on east gable. The three-span **Altnaharra Bridge** over the River Mudale, c.1815, Thomas Telford, carries the Parliamentary road to Tongue.

Beaton

Altnaharra Primary School and schoolhouse

STRATH FLEET & ROGART
Strath Fleet lies east of Lairg carrying the A839 and the railway to Loch Fleet and The Mound. Both valley and hills are scattered with many individually named farms, settlements and crofting townships together comprising the widespread parish of Rogart.

Below *Acheilidh, one of many scattered townships in Strath Fleet; white railway cottage (rear) fronts sunken railway line linking Inverness and north.* Bottom *Pulpit, St Callan's Church, Rogart*

Beaton

St Callan's (St Colin) Church of Scotland, 1777, probably James Boag
Simple whitewashed rectangular kirk with gableted bellcote, 1857, by William Fowler. Its regular south elevation is lit by narrow windows and served by paired doors. Sited on high ground with panoramic views of Rogart and enclosed by walled burial ground with morthouse. The interior has been recast (perhaps by William Fowler in 1857); handsome pulpit with corniced sounding board probably dating from George Alexander's repair work in the church, 1817, when it would have been sited in the centre of the south wall, lit by the flanking windows. Restored 1955 (colour page 50). Former gabled **manse**, dated 1883, William Fowler, enclosed by fine drystone coped wall.

Historic Scotland

Free Church, Pitfure, 1844
Austere grey rubble rectangular church with
gable entrance; ornate cast-iron gallery front to
otherwise plain interior, perhaps fitted in 1899,
during alterations by J Pond Macdonald. The
group, in its sheltered bosky setting, includes
former FC school and handsome regularly
fronted grey granite **manse**, c.1845.

Church of Scotland, Rovie, 1909-10,
R J Macbeth
Former UF Church. Simple rubble building with
principal gable lit by triple lancets; neighbouring
dormered **manse**, 1910, also R J Macbeth.
Acheillie Lodge, dated 1884, was the school
serving the western end of Strath Fleet.
Stylistically very much in the Sutherland school
pattern. **Tressady Lodge**, late 18th-century
core with various additions including one dated
1886: rambling but pleasant homogeneous group.

Above *Acheillie Lodge*.
Right *Tressady Lodge, Rogart*

Morvich Lodge: Below *Plan and
elevation.* Bottom right *As built by
Lord Stafford (1st Duke of
Sutherland)*

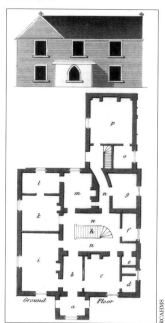

Morvich Lodge, 1812, George Alexander
Two-storey, white harled with ashlar margins;
plain box-like porch enlivened by pointed-
headed window; unusual triple-gabled north-
east elevation. Sited on a rise overlooking
Strath Fleet, the house was built by Lord
Stafford (later Duke of Sutherland) *for his
occasional residence* and subsequently let to his
notorious factor, Patrick Sellar.

Beaton

About this toun, along the sea coast, there are the fairest and largest linkes or green feilds of any pairt of Scotland, fitt for archery, goffing, ryding, and all other exercise; they doe surpasse the feilds of Montrose or St Andrews.
Sir Robert Gordon, 1630

Dornoch, general view

DORNOCH

Dornoch, ancient capital of Sutherland and a pleasant town centred on its historic 13th-century cathedral, now the parish church. This is sited between High Street and Castle Street, the latter flanked by some fine buildings, tree-lined and widening to form a dignified yet intimate setting, a rare and little-known gem, quite magical when floodlit.

Contrasting with the main streets and larger houses are groups of cottages flanked by narrow lanes which fade into leafy footpaths offering glimpses of the cathedral and panoramic views over the Dornoch Firth. Hotels fringe the golf links, and villas with substantial gardens overlook the sea, for the *fairest and largest linkes* so suitable for *goffing and other exercise* have long brought visitors and summer residents, particularly after the opening of the Dornoch Light Railway in June 1902. This linked the town with the Highland Railway station at The Mound, a distance of seven miles, the line following the southern shore of Loch Fleet. It closed after 58 years of service in June 1960.

Sir Robert Gordon (1580-1656), 4th son of Alexander, 12th Earl of Sutherland: academic, landowner, courtier, lawyer and tutor or guardian to his nephew, John, 14th Earl. Sutherland was Sir Robert's first love: he relieved the estate of debt in 1621 *for he cared so little of his own compared with Sutherland.* He wrote the massive *Genealogical History of Earldom of Sutherland, from its Origin to year 1630. A most constant performer of his word and promise, when he had once ingadged the same; sincere and honest in all his proceedings, and so reputed generallie be all men . . . He may be justly called a rare instrument in Sutherland for the weill of that familie and for the flourishing state of the commonwealth in that countie.*
Gilbert Gordon of Sallagh, 1656

Dornoch Cathedral was built by Gilbert de Moravia, Bishop of Caithness (which included Sutherland), at his own expense. Noted for his wisdom, courage and administrative ability, Gilbert became bishop in 1222, moving the centre of the diocese from Halkirk, Caithness, to Dornoch two years later, dying there in 1245. He was a relative of Hugh Freskyne de Moravia, father of the 1st Earl of Sutherland, from whom he received both Skelbo and Skibo castles. When first built, there were many similarities in plan and measurement between Dornoch and Elgin Cathedrals (see *Moray* in this series), not surprising for Bishop Gilbert had been Archdeacon of Moray, 1206-7, and was involved in the preparation, 1216-24, of Elgin Cathedral in its first form.

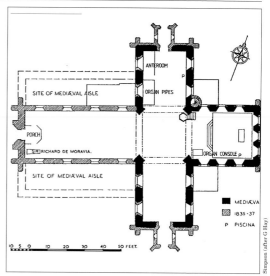

SITE OF MEDIÆVAL AISLE

ANTEROOM P

ORGAN PIPES

PORCH

SIR RICHARD DE MORAVIA.

SITE OF MEDIÆVAL AISLE

ORGAN CONSOLE P

■ MEDIÆVA

▨ 1835-37

P PISCINA

10 5 0   10   20   30   40   50 FEET.

Simpson (after G Hay)

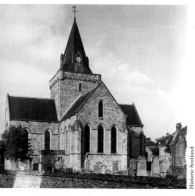

Right Plan, Dornoch Cathedral.
Above Dornoch Cathedral, east

Historic Scotland

In 1835-7, Elizabeth, Duchess and Countess of Sutherland, undertook what she described as a 'plain & correct restoration' [of Dornoch Cathedral] . . . Drawings for the scheme were produced by William Burn; but the Duchess, disliking his 'modern gothic in bad taste' and 'useless plans of ornaments', dismissed him before work began, and the executed designs were by Alexander Coupar, the Superintendent of Works on the Sutherland estates, assisted by William Leslie. Advice was provided by Francis Chantrey and sketches by the Duchess.
John Gifford, *The Buildings of Scotland: Highlands and Islands,* 1992

4 **Dornoch Cathedral**, from 1224
Chancel, transepts and tower were ready for worship by 1239 and the nave apparently built by the 15th century. After serious damage by fire in 1570 the chancel and transepts were reroofed, and the tower probably completed in its present form in 1616; broached spire, 1728. Complete restoration, 1835-7, by Alexander Coupar, Superintendent of Works for the Sutherland Estates, assisted by William Leslie whose work was influenced by earlier unexecuted plans by William Burn. Clock installed, 1924.

The cruciform Gothic cathedral has a central tower with corbelled wallhead and open angle bartizans in the Scottish tower-house tradition, the red sandstone walls glowing when lit by warm sunlight. The broached, dark slated spire, in perfect proportion to tower and body, elevates the cathedral above houses and enclosing trees as a dignified architectural riposte to the bulky height of the neighbouring *castle*. The four-bay buttressed nave, three-bay chancel and two-bay transepts have tall narrow lancets linked by continuous stringcourses. A fine intersecting traceried window lights the west gable, the east gable wall pierced by tall triple lights. Entry is by a south porch of 1835-7 or west gable doorway.

Essentially the building is that restored in 1835-7 at the expense of Elizabeth, Duchess/Countess of Sutherland. Internally, Alexander Coupar's cruciform plan respects the medieval structure of the chancel (raised to accommodate the Sutherland vault), transept and tower but rebuilt a narrower, aisleless nave in place of the roofless aisled structure, arguably more suited to the architectural form and present use of the building. Medieval fabric survives in the chancel, the eastern transept walls and the lower part of the western transept walls. Coupar copied the shape and tracery of the former west gable window, but shortened it to accommodate the west doorway. The crenellated wallhead of the central tower and the spire of 1728 were rebuilt, but appear to follow closely the original form (colour page 50).

Dornoch Cathedral: Above *Fragment of 15th-century nave column.* Left *Chancel and crossing plaster vaulting, 1835-7.* Below *Cluster column at crossing.* Bottom *Tombstone of 1790*

The dignified lofty interior retains its medieval Gothic character, the central crossing tower supported by cluster piers carved from Dornoch stone, restored c.1925, their capitals and arches of Embo stone. Immediately west of the tower crossing fragments of filleted moulded columns are exposed in mural recesses; these supported the 15th-century nave arcade. The soaring, plaster, groined ceiling *vaulting*, rising from simple corbel tables (brackets), is the work of Alexander Coupar, entirely appropriate and in keeping with the masonry vaulting probably envisaged by the medieval builders. Coupar, however, plastered the walls and ceiling in 1835-7; this plaster was removed in 1925 to reveal the rubble walling.

There are some interesting commemorative plaques; the recumbent effigy of a knight in chain mail in the south-west corner of the nave is said to be Richard de Moravia, died c.1245. Richly carved octagonal pulpit and communion table, which together with the pews, date from 1911.

Nineteenth- and 20th-century lustrous stained glass, including Morris & Co, Percy

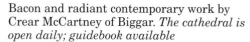

Above *Cast-iron fountain.*
Right *Dornoch Academy*

Bacon and radiant contemporary work by
Crear McCartney of Biggar. *The cathedral is
open daily; guidebook available*

Of note in the cathedral burial ground is the
ell stone, used to regulate the measurement of
cloth (colour page 50). The **burgh cross** is
close by in High Street while in Castle Street
there is a charming cast-iron **fountain**, 1892,
the design straight out of MacFarlane's of
Glasgow catalogue. Some of the surrounding
houses occupy sites of medieval clergy houses.
Unlike Elgin (see *Moray* in this series) Dornoch
had no formal Chanonry separating the clergy
residences from those of the laity.

Evelix Road links Dornoch with the A9.
Dornoch Academy, 1961, Eric Hall &
Partners; series of single, two- and three-storey
pale-harled blocks, the upper floors supported
by stilt-like columns to project over covered
walkway. The range contrasts with the gabled
red sandstone neighbouring **school** of 1844.

*Castle Street approaching city centre
from west*

Castle Street
Main approach from the west, lined with late
18th- and 19th-century houses until it broadens
to create an open space around the cathedral.

5 Former **United Free Church**, 1908,
R J Macbeth
Now parish church hall. Quirky Gothic Revival.
Well sited on corner plot, red sandstone with
liberal use of contrasting pale ashlar dressings;
stalwart gabled entrance front delineated by
giant pilasters; four-bay buttressed long
elevations, slate roof with ridge crowned with
squat ventilator.

Clydesdale Bank (former Town & County
Bank), 1893, A Maitland & Sons
Plain, somewhat conventional bank building,

the symmetrical two-storey front enhanced by simple pilastered doorpiece and tripartite (three-light) ground-floor windows.

Most houses in Castle Street are plain, their simple regularity adding dignity to the principal entry of this ancient burgh. **The Deanery**, c.1840, on the site of the pre-Reformation deanery, has a pilastered and pedimented frontage, the centre first-floor window topped by a pretty shell-motif lintel. Mini-obelisk end finials enhance the wallhead.

Above Clydesdale Bank. Left The Deanery

6 **Dornoch Castle Hotel**, from c.1500
Built as an Episcopal palace, substantially reconstructed after fire in 1570. Tall, imposing five-storey bartizaned and crowstepped tower-house. Slightly lower 16th-century south wing with massive wallhead chimney-stack. The north elevation, fronting the street, was extended in the 19th century. Later walled courtyard entrance from street leads to main hotel entry and garden. The dominant, baronial exterior of the building contributes much to the townscape. Other than a low vaulted former kitchen, nothing remains of the original internal layout.

Dornoch Castle Hotel

After the Reformation the building was transferred to John, Earl of Sutherland, by Bishop Robert Stewart. From 1814 to 1850 it served as court-room and county jail, when it was graced with the dual Stafford/Sutherland armorial. In 1859-60 William Fowler altered the building, with advice from George Devey, as a residence for the Sheriff of Sutherland. By 1881 the castle had been *refitted and refurbished as a quaint dwelling place for English sportsmen* and it continues a similar role as a hotel (colour page 51).

Above *Jail, rear elevation with baronial details and small cell windows.* Right *Jail (left), Court-house (centre), Dornoch Castle Hotel (right)*

Below *Former Post Office.* Bottom *Carnegie Building*

County Buildings & **Court-house**, 1840-50, Thomas Brown
Crowstepped and gabled, with arcaded ground floor and first-floor court-room lit by long triple lights. The adjacent **Jail**, 1842-50, also Thomas Brown, is flanked by the later **drill hall**, 1896-7, both with baronial embellishments. The symmetrical frontage of the jail with advanced wings and large windows gives little indication of the building's true function; however, a glance at the side and rear elevations reveals small cell windows. It is now a '**jail museum**' and well worth a visit for the quality of the masonry, the interior layout and its fittings; the adjoining drill hall is a craft centre. *Open all the year round, except for the Christmas period; guidebook available*

[7] Former **Post Office**, *c.*1900, probably A Maitland & Sons
Delightful, asymmetrical gabled building in red sandstone now housing the Tourist Information Centre and a solicitor's office. This enjoys a corner site and offers an attractive return frontage to Station Road. In contrast, the dark rubble **Free Church of Scotland**, 1844, renovated 1896, is a gaunt Gothic building with long windows and pinnacled entrance gable. **Police Station**, 1985, Gordon Falconer, box-like and something of an architectural misfit, though the reddish external cladding attempts to blend with the neighbourhood.

Station Road
Carnegie Building housing **Council Chamber** & **Library**, 1907, occupies corner of Station Road and High Street. Civic dignity and literary philanthropy combined as a substantial gabled two-storey building of dullish red Embo stone. Council Chamber & Library share a hood-moulded, round-headed main entrance, both lit by large mullioned windows.

Netherwood, 1850-60, retains its characteristic Scottish lying-pane (horizontal) glazing in all windows except later canted dormers: pleasant regular frontage with wide shallow-arched recess housing central doorway. Balconied **Tochallt Lodge**, c.1985, MacDonald Associates, two storeys with deep-eaved roof in a wooded setting: a kindly blend of traditional materials and modern design. Former **station, Dornoch Light Railway**, 1902, a simple timber building with piended roof, now a shop. The platform area behind is landscaped while the former railway yard provides the site for light industrial buildings. **St Michael's Well**, 1832, simple inscribed roadside plinth north of the former station.

Above *Former station, Dornoch Light Railway; wood studded walls, sturdy chimney-stacks and piended slate roof all add up to a traditional Highland building of its period.*
Left *Netherwood*

St Michael's Well: *According to local historians, this stone marks not a well but a voter's ingenuity . . . . The 1832 Reform Act (Scotland) required that voters should live within 7 miles of the nearest Burgh boundary. The Sutherland estate's factor, George Gunn, lived at Rhives near Golspie which he thought was beyond the required distance. Nothing daunted he had this stone erected, marked and placed near enough Rhives to allow him to retain his vote and seat on the Dornoch Town Council.*
Dornoch Heritage Society

Above *St Michael's Well, 1832.* Left *Tochallt Lodge.* Below *St Michael's*

Schoolhill

Land between St Michael's and St Finnbarr's Episcopal Church *east of the burn* was apportioned to the medieval cathedral dignitaries for manses for Treasurer, Chancellor and Precentor. **St Michael's**, 1802 or 1807 (faint datestone), on the site of the pre-Reformation cathedral Treasurer's manse, ruinous by 1801. The regular two-storey house is flanked by lower wings. Large segmental-

headed hearth in east wing may survive from
earlier building.

8 **St Finnbarr's Episcopal Church**, 1912,
Alexander Ross
Simple buttressed Gothic church in Ross
Episcopalian style. Pointed-headed windows
light a modest interior, and dignity added by
the ridge flèche and 1966 timber porch. The
new stone church succeeded the plain *iron and
wood chapel* (Speirs & Co, Glasgow) erected
near the station in 1909, the first Episcopal
chapel in Sutherland since 1689. Aptly the site,
once associated with the medieval cathedral,
remains in ecclesiastical use.

9 **Gilchrist Square**, early 19th century
Pleasant low, L-plan terrace range of cottages
backing on to narrow street. From here a path
leads up to **Cnocan-Lobht**, a street
overlooking the firth and lined with Victorian
villas on one side, fringed on the other by bosky
gardens descending steeply to Castle Street.
Burghfield House Hotel, late 19th century;
substantial mansion crowned with a square
baronial tower surmounted by circular turret.
Of note amongst other villas in the street is the
crowstepped gabled **Cathedral Manse** (Tigh-
na-Mara), *c*.1880, standing in a generous
garden enclosed by walls and railings.

10 **Links House**, Kennedy Road, *c*.1844,
James Raeburn
Handsome former manse with good moulded
window margins and wide angle pilasters. A
standard design by James Raeburn for Free
Church manses. **Royal Golf Hotel**, formerly
The Grange, *c*.1896, J R Rhind, two-storey
villa, porch (1897) flanked by protuberant
round bay windows rising full height; deep-

The Grange photographed in 1896. Now Royal Golf Hotel

eaved roofs topped by decorative iron thistles. The house originally belonged to the Holderness family, which included some notable golfers.

11 **Dornoch Hotel**, 1902-4, Cameron & Burnett Large, slightly institutional, cream-harled hotel, the roofscape enlivened with dormers, half-timbered gables and pottery finials. The hotel was built by the Highland Railway for summer visitors after the construction of the rail link from The Mound to Dornoch in 1902.

Opposite from top: St Finnbarr's Episcopal Church, 1912, porch, 1966; Cottages, Gilchrist Square; Cathedral Manse; Design for Free Church manse, James Raeburn 'drawn and presented by Robert R Raeburn, 1845'. Bottom right Links House

Dornoch Hotel: overlooking golf links and sea, and built to accommodate summer visitors

Earl's Cross Road lined with pleasant 20th-century houses, some of modest size, built against a woodland backdrop, hazy with bluebells in spring. **Earl's Cross House**, allegedly 1913; two-storey house with harled walls under heavy brown stone slate roof with broad chimney-stacks. The house hugs its sloping site, blending into the hillside in Edwardian rural revival manner. On the links below, the **Earl's Cross**, possibly 15th century: rough stone shaft with a shaped head. It is said to be a *march stone* separating church lands from those of the Earls of Sutherland and to identify a market place. Legend persists that it is the site of a battle fought, c.1245, between the 1st Earl of Sutherland and marauding invaders.

Earl's Cross House: deep eaves, heavy brown slate roof, squat chimney-stacks, stylistic characteristics of the vernacular revival in architecture

Above and right *Embo House c.1790.*
Below *Detail of sandstone dressings
and original lead rainwater pipe
with decorative head*

We arrived [at Embo House] . . .
*before it got dark, so that I had an
opportunity of seeing in fair daylight
the most elegant mansion I have ever
witnessed, with the exception of
Dunrobin Castle . . . Embo House
was constructed very much after the
fashion of the houses in the New
Town of Edinburgh.*
The Revd Donald Sage, 1801

Embo was owned by the Gordons of
Embo; in the 18th century The Old
House of Embo was a six-roomed
house, whose last owner, Sir John
Gordon, died leaving a large family
and many debts. His principal
creditor was Robert Hume Gordon,
who made money from a plantation
in Jamaica; he bought the property
between 1777-90 and built the
present mansion, principally to
entertain and impress supporters
when he stood for Parliament
against the candidate supported by
the Sutherlands of Dunrobin.

12 **EMBO**
Embo House, *c.*1790
Elegant symmetrical house, harled with fine
sandstone margins and quoins, the centre
three-storey block joined to two-storey wings
by slightly set-back single-bay passage link,
each lit by a round-headed window
accentuated by chunky rusticated dressings.
The centre entrance is reached by a flight of
stairs, its lintel and those of the flanking
windows linked by a deep sandstone band.
The centre bay rises into a nepus (wallhead)
gable topped by a chimney and defined by a
band of sandstone as an attempt to turn this
vernacular gablet, so characteristic of the
Highland laird's house, into a classical
pediment. The west range contained kitchen
with segmental-headed hearth with reset
armorial dated 1657. The arms are those of
Sir Robert Gordon of Embo and his wife Jean
Leslie. There were two detached (*c.*1790)
pavilions sited symmetrically at rear of house;
one is now incorporated in the garage. The
present owner has planted the road verges
with daffodils, a joy in springtime.

The Embo road was once the main highway
linking Dornoch with Golspie at Little Ferry;
the road crossing of Loch Fleet upstream at
The Mound achieved in 1818 and from then
on this old route became secondary and quiet.

Embo village, originally a fishing settlement, consists mainly of parallel rows of single-storey cottages.

SKELBO

Skelbo Castle, 13th-15th centuries
Ruinous, crowning a hilltop overlooking Loch Fleet and the sea beyond. The castle was enclosed by a curtain wall, probably 13th century, with a 15th-century keep in the north corner.

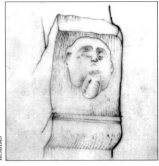

Left *Reconstruction of Old Skelbo House*. Top and above *Decorative skewputts*

Just below the castle stands **Old Skelbo House**, *c.*1600, an unusually long rectangular crowstepped two-storey dwelling, the ground floor a continuously vaulted undercroft, the windowed first floor with a blocked entrance with moulded jambs. Excavations have revealed byre drainage in the vaulted ground floor, ample evidence that cattle were housed here. There were extensive 18th-century repairs and a later east gable doorway served by a ramp. The decorative mask skewputts, a man with bulging cheeks and a lady wearing a Tudor ruff, are noteworthy and charming. Now in a sorry state of repair, this building deserves restoration as an unusual semi-fortified, prestigious farmhouse or *bastel*, recognised in the Borders but rare in the Highlands; a transition between the traditional vertical tower-house and later laird's house. Old Skelbo House provided a greater degree of domestic comfort than the medieval castle, but the first-floor living quarters reached by withdrawable ladder retained a defensive characteristic (colour page 51).

Skelbo Castle and Old Skelbo House, early 18th-century drawing

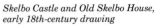

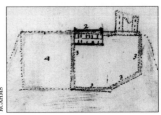

Skelbo Farm Steading

RCAHMS

Skelbo Farm Steading, 1853, after a design by James Loch (see p.58). Impressive, long nine-bay crowstepped range with central bellcote.

PRONCY, CAMBUSAVIE & TORBOLL
Proncy Castle
Stronghold of the Gordons of Proncy, now merely a mound near the farm of that name, surrounded by crofting settlements. At **Proncycroy**, just off the A9, stands the **Proncy Stone**, a memorial to Sheriff Hugh MacCulloch (1741-1809) of Kirkton (see p.41) drowned in the Meikle Ferry disaster, 1809, one of 99 people who died when the ferry capsized.

Northern Times

Right & below *Cambusavie Hospital*

Beaton

. . . new Composite Iron and Wood
***Infectious Diseases Hospital** to be erected at Cambusavie, near the Mound Station, Highland Railway . . . The building, which will be constructed of a wooden framework, covered externally with galvanised corrugated iron, and internally with tongued and grooved matchboarding on the Speirs patent system of airspaced walls, to ensure comfort and durability . . .*
The Northern Times, 5 April 1906

Cambusavie Hospital, from 1906
Prominent on the bare hillside (originally the Sutherland County Infectious Diseases Hospital), a cluster of green and cream painted corrugated-iron, wood-lined hutted wards manufactured by Speirs & Co, Glasgow, each pavilion isolating a different illness. The hospital housed geriatric patients during its final years; closed 1989. **Cambusmore Lodge** is a many-gabled, much-extended house of diverse builds unified by attractive bargeboards.

Torboll, early 19th century
L-plan farmhouse of more than one build on a commanding site overlooking Strath Fleet. White harled with regular four-window frontage: long catslide roof to rear wing. A Neolithic chambered **tomb** indicates the antiquity of the place: the name is of Norse

origin, suggesting *Thor's steading*. Close by, the **Torboll waterfall** is an elaborate, 19th-century rubble **salmon ladder**, 34m (110ft) long and one of the earliest of its kind. This *ladder*, in effect a series of man-made pools, enabled the fish to bypass the falls and swim upstream to spawn.

THE MOUND
The Mound, 1813-16, Thomas Telford
Dam carrying causeway and bridge crosses Loch Fleet, replacing the treacherous ferry crossing at Little Ferry. The pent-up waters of Loch Fleet are drained by an impressive series of sluice gates (four in 1816, increased to six by Joseph Mitchell, 1837) in the six-span bridge. Each arch is fitted with a wooden non-returnable flap valve which prevents the sea water from flowing up-river, while allowing the fresh water to drain away. A system of chains and pulleys open the sluices, the winding gear housed in small stone huts each side of the bridge. The considerable cost of this enterprise, which created new, well-drained land besides improving communications, was £12,500 of which the Marquis of Stafford (later Duke of Sutherland) contributed £8000 (colour page 50). Early 19th-century **custodian's house** on the north bank, deep eaved with hood-moulded windows; extensively restored 1988, R I Beaton. The Mound bridge bypassed by a concrete flyover constructed 1988-9.

The **Dornoch Light Railway**, linking Dornoch with the Highland Railway, ran parallel to the road along The Mound, 1902-60: the rails have been removed, the track is still visible, flanked by occasional linesmen's bothies.

Salmon ladder, Torboll

Linesmen's bothy, Dornoch Light Railway, the track just visible in a field beside Loch Fleet

KIRKTON, DRUMMUIE & LITTLE FERRY
Kirkton, *c.*1810
Symmetrical harled two-storey house, enlivened by long and short detailing and with later wing. Built by a lawyer, Robert MacKid, Sheriff-Substitute for Sutherland. The prefix 'Kirk' is a reminder that this was the site of the

Drummuie

The Sutherland Technical School was established in 1903 by Millicent, Duchess of Sutherland, on land given by her husband, the 4th Duke, together with £8000, Andrew Carnegie subscribing a further £5000. The well-appointed school was innovatory, the first of its kind in Scotland, providing free residential education for the sons of crofters from isolated communities in the Highlands and Islands. The boys were aged 13-16; the aim was that they would return home better educated and more competent farmers though many achieved success in other walks of life. The building now serves as the technical annexe to Golspie High School.

Above *Elevation, Sutherland Technical School.* Right *Sutherland Technical School*

Little Ferry Girnal House

medieval Kilmallie (Culmaily) parish church dedicated to St Maliew (Moluag), *ruynous* (sic) *to the ground* in 1619 when Sir Robert Gordon built a new church in Golspie in *the midst of the parish and neir* (sic) *the house of Dounrobin.*

Drummuie, *c.*1809
A handsome and commodious house.
Symmetrical two-storey central block flanked by lower wings, which until the 1960s was the headmaster's house for the neighbouring school. **Sutherland Technical School**, 1903, J M Dick Peddie, Scottish Renaissance school, originally for 40 boarders. Tall, crowstepped, gabled, E-plan frontage with centre advanced bay; above the entrance is inscribed *Let there be Light* together with the initials MFS for Millicent Fanny Sutherland. Generous provision of multi-pane windows ensures a well-lit interior.

Little Ferry
On the north bank of the fast-flowing River Fleet and, until 1818, the principal but hazardous crossing of Loch Fleet for the north/south route. Now a pleasant backwater, the frontage lined with cottages and houses of *c.*1800. Large early 19th-century **icehouse** with winged frontage typical of the Sutherland estate (colour page 51).

Little Ferry Girnal House,
early 18th century
Sutherland estate store or girnal converted to five dwellings in 1859, probably by William Fowler, when its usefulness as a store for rents-in-kind was over. Sited conveniently by the shore, it stored mostly grain and meal exported to urban markets by boat for

conversion into cash. The original rectangular warehouse, with crowstepped gables and end forestairs, acquired a pleasant slightly English gabled frontage, multi-light windows and tall rear and ridge chimney-stacks in a manner reminiscent of alterations designed the previous year by George Devey for Big Barns, Strathsteven (see p.57). Internal alterations to single holiday home, 1957, R I Beaton.

Golspie, a linear town sited between sea and hill, dominated by the statue of 1st Duke of Sutherland on Ben Bhragaidh

GOLSPIE

Bounded by sea and hill, Golspie's building line follows the gentle curve of the shore on one hand, diminishing as the land rises to the enclosing hills north and west. Of these, Ben Bhragaidh is dominant, crowned by a colossal statue of the 1st Duke of Sutherland (by Sir Francis Chantrey, 1837), surveying the village below. With shops, banks, hospital and a large secondary school, it provides services for the surrounding countryside.

The north/south A9 runs the length of the village as Main Street and Old Bank Road, lined mostly by simple red stone houses and shops. Most buildings date from the 19th century onwards: the distinctive Sutherland style is evident in the Sutherland Arms Hotel, estate cottages and drill hall. Fishing was once centred near the pier at the south end of the village, fishermen and their families living in Shore and Church Streets.

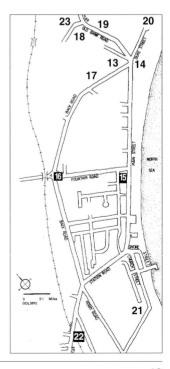

13 **St Andrew's Church of Scotland**, 1736-7
On site of medieval chapel of St Andrew succeeded in 1619 by parish church translated from Kirkton of Kilmallie (Culmaily); south aisle added 1751; bellcote 1774 housing 1696 bell. Enclosed in its walled burial ground, cruciform and white harled, gently dignified St Andrew's is the most atmospheric of Highland

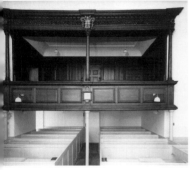

St Andrew's Church: Top Pulpit.
Above *Laird's loft*

The Sutherland *laird's loft* was made by Kenneth Sutherland, joiner at Dunrobin, his account totalling *Fourty one pd. three Shill and Sevenpence.* He also made the pulpit and sounding board for which he was paid £2 by the Kirk Session.

18th-century kirks. The steeply pitched crowstepped roof is enhanced with ball finials and apex bellcote, and the small, regularly disposed sash windows filled with clear glass. The rear wing houses the retiring room behind the *laird's loft* with a forestair providing private access to the church for Earls (later Dukes) of Sutherland of Dunrobin Castle (colour page 51).

Inside the simple white-plastered walls have few mural monuments, the floor paved with stone flags, only carpeted *c*.1990. The panelled pews were installed in 1954, the design by Dr George Hay closely following the original. This plain, light interior is dominated by the impressive 1738 pulpit, the carved backboard and hexagonal sounding board by Kenneth Sutherland, also responsible for the imposing *laird's loft* of a year later. This *loft* has an enriched entablature with armorial supported by slender Corinthian columns; the front and interior are panelled and the plain plaster ceiling coved. The rear retiring room hearth is served by a neat corniced apex chimney. There was no other heating in the church until recently, the closely packed congregation being expected to generate their own warmth!

14 **Ford Park**, 1825-7, William Alexander
Former Church of Scotland manse sited at corner of Main and Duke Streets. Symmetrically fronted, white-harled two-storey house with porch of pleasant early 19th-century proportions standing within a walled garden. There was an earlier manse on the site, conveniently close to the church and with an outlook over Golspie and the sea.

Main Street follows the sweep of the shore to which it is linked by footpaths squeezed between

Main Street: James Fraser's shop (right), 1906

the buildings lining the street. **The Hollies,**
*c.*1830-40, is a deep-eaved villa; **The Cottage,**
1868, paired with **Newton** (former police
station), 1866, and **Glen Coul** with **Gairloch** of
about the same date, are of red sandstone and
gabled in the distinctive Sutherland estate style
of the period. On the opposite side of the street,
the **post office,** *c.*1910, probably David Horne,
is built of grey Clynelish stone, its mural post-
box graced with a curved cornice. In marked
contrast, **Golspie High School,** 1962-3, Reiach
& Hall, is a flat-roofed, angular building with
some brickwork to relieve the extensively glazed
frontage. Associated **swimming pool,** 1972,
Allan Ross & Allan.

Above *Post office, c.1910.*
Left *Golspie High School*

15 **James Fraser's shop,** corner of Fountain
Road, dated 1906, David Horne
Edwardian, asymmetrical composition with
original shop fenestration, the first-floor
domestic quarters lit by wide windows and an
oriel, the street elevation enhanced by a shaped
gable. Monogram AA, for Archibald Argo, who
commissioned David Horne, a local architect, to
design his speculative building. The large
public clock, erected 1901, was financed by
funds raised in 1887 to mark Queen Victoria's
Diamond Jubilee. It projects from the (YMCA)
hall, also 1901, with red sandstone street gable
lit by long windows.

95 Main Street, 1867, William Fowler
Tall, former Co-op with a strong Scottish
Renaissance flavour, its curved corner corbelled
out at wallhead as a square, crowstepped cap-
house; a circular stair-turret projects at the rear.

Fountain Road
Flanked by villas and terminated by a square
16 canopied memorial **fountain** to Elizabeth,
Duchess and Countess of Sutherland, designed,
*c.*1850-1, by Sir Charles Barry. Former **United
Free Church,** 1906, L Bisset. Gothic with
square tower crowned by slated spire; shining
pale grey local Clynelish stone. **Moray House,**
1859-60, George Devey. Tudor with mullioned

Former United Free Church

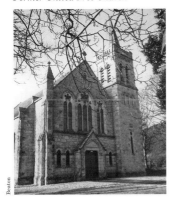

45

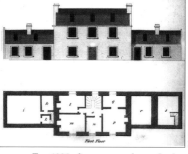

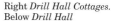

Top *1930s former secondary school with metal window frames.* Middle *Scroll finials, gable-end brackets and shaped chimney-stacks, Ben Bhraggie Hotel.* Above *Sutherland Arms*

windows, advanced gabled porch and tall diagonal chimney-stacks. **Lochnagarry**, 1868, probably William Fowler; grey Clynelish stone in distinctive local villa pattern. Projecting canted bay windows, deep eaves below fishscale slate roof and gabled porch.

Back Road

Gabled red stone **primary school**: centre block, 1841, Alexander Coupar, inscribed with a decorative S for Sutherland and apex bellcote. Wings, 1875, William Fowler (west) and 1892 (east). Long single-storey, 10-bay 17 **former secondary school**, 1938, E W Brannan, with big multi-paned metal-framed windows lighting the south-facing classrooms.

Old Bank Road

Ben Bhraggie Hotel, dated 1829 & 1886 Former Town & County Bank, notable for its top-heavy wallhead dormers decorated with chunky attenuated scrolls. **Macleod House**, 1877, William Fowler, was built as the Aberdeen Town & County Bank; large gabled villa with full-height canted bay window and a porch with roof supported by squat columns (colour page 51).

18 **Sutherland Arms**, 1808, George Alexander Dignified two-storey, russet-red inn, the wing of 1826-7 creating an L-plan. Built by the Sutherland estate to serve travellers on the new road: much-altered interior with fine 1808 datestone bearing the double arms of Stafford and Sutherland. **Drill Hall Cottages**, 1896, delightful, with mock timber framing to evoke the Stafford connection with the English West Midlands building traditions. The cottages take their name from the large, timber-clad 19 Volunteer, later Territorial Army, **Drill Hall**, 1892, L Bisset. Impressive structure with

Right *Drill Hall Cottages.* Below *Drill Hall*

timber-studded walls and corrugated-iron roof. In contrast is the small, late 19th-century rustic timber **shop** (now hairdresser) where wools and tweeds, spun and woven locally, were sold under the auspices of the Highland Home Industries.

Duke Street

Charming earlier 19th-century row of cottages, the dormers fitted with sliding sash windows, another Sutherland estate hallmark (colour page 50). Equally characteristic grey rubble **estate & architect's offices**, 1894, style of William Fowler, adorned with armorial. **Tower** 20 **Lodge**, from 1865, an earlier L-plan house remodelled for the Estate Surveyor, William Fowler. Romantic asymmetrical, single- and two-storey L-plan dwelling with porch in re-entrant angle. South gable terminated by a conical-roofed two-storey tower added by Devey. The first-floor room (originally the smoking room) lit by pointed-headed windows and reached by outer forestair curving around the east wall. The entrance at the base of the tower led to the former office. The house still serves as the estate factor's home. Internal remodelling, 1962, by R I Beaton.

Rustic shop, Old Bank Road

The Sutherland, later Highland, Home Industries were established by Harriet, 3rd Duchess of Sutherland, in 1849 to promote the sale of local tweeds and woollens to bring some earnings where they were most needed, into the homes of small farmers and crofters. The scheme was revitalised in 1886 by her energetic and philanthropic daughter-in-law, Millicent, who raised the standard of design and manufacture. Millicent toured the Hebrides in 1896 and 1898 in her husband's yacht, offered prizes for quality and encouraged sales amongst her wealthy friends. Five years later 500 families in the Highlands and Islands were gainfully employed in this activity.

George Devey (1820-86), prolific country-house London architect, was introduced to the Duke of Sutherland by the Duke's cousin, Lord Granville. *In the hands of such men as George Devey . . . the vernacular, or regional and homely, architecture of the sixteenth, seventeenth and early eighteenth centuries was adapted to the needs of country-house design . . . [Devey's] practice was sustained by the recommendations of his satisfied clients . . . His houses attempt to give the appearance of having grown up gradually over a number of years, even centuries. He used local materials and so handled them as to give the impression that the craftsman rather than the architect determined their use.* Roger Dixon & Stefan Muthesius, *Victorian Architecture*, 1978; also Jill Allibone, *George Devey, 1820-1886*, 1991

Tower Lodge: Above left Asymmetrical design by George Devey. Left Sketch by George Devey, 1858-60

Above *Free Church*. Right *Golspie Station; SR monogram for Sutherland Railway. Arcaded veranda, bull-faced masonry and solid chimney-stacks are all characteristic of Sutherland building at this time*

Church Street & Shore Street

Once the heart of the Gaelic-speaking fisher-town. Church Street is lined with low, single-storey former fishermen's cottages. **Free Church**, 1844, uncompromisingly plain red sandstone kirk. Former gabled **manse** now a hotel.

22 **Golspie Station**, 1868, William Fowler
Handsome gabled station-house with dormers and roof sweeping over veranda supported by timber arcade. Very much in the Sutherland idiom, hardly surprising for the Duke of Sutherland was entirely responsible for the stretch of rail between Golspie and Helmsdale (The Duke of Sutherland's Railway; note the plaque monogrammed SR). Regrettably Golspie Station is now *unmanned* and the handsome building devoid of human activity.

The railway is carried over the Golspie Burn on a high single-span arched **bridge**, 1870-1, Murdoch Paterson, in a wooded glen to the north of the village. This burn provided the water power for **Golspie Mill**, 1863, on the site of an earlier mill. Fine three-storey, five-bay red rubble building with a large kiln projecting at rear. The largest mill in Sutherland, it continues to work on a small scale (colour page 52).

Below *Statue of 1st Duke of Sutherland by Sir Francis Chantrey, 1837, dominates Golspie from Ben Bhragaidh*. Bottom *Golspie Mill*

Beaton

Beaton

Beaton

Beaton

Beaton

Top *Strathcarron and Gruinards Lodge*. Middle left *Matheson Memorial, Lairg*. Left *Brae Doune Bridge over River Oykel*. Middle above *Old Shin Bridge, Invershin*. Above *Croick Church*

49

Beaton

Beaton

Beaton

Beaton

Beaton

Top *Rogart with St Callan's Church in foreground.* Middle left *Dornoch Cathedral and fountain.* Bottom left *Ell stone, Dornoch Cathedral.* Middle right *1-2 Duke Street, Golspie: note sliding sash windows in dormers.* Bottom right *Sluice gates, The Mound*

Opposite: Top left *Skelbo Castle and Old Skelbo House.* Top right *Dornoch Castle Hotel.* Middle left *St Andrew's Church, Golspie.* Middle right *Macleod House (former bank).* Bottom *Little Ferry and Loch Fleet*

Beaton

Beaton

Beaton

Beaton

Beaton

Beaton

Beaton

Beaton

Beaton

Beaton

Top *Helmsdale*. Middle right
Icehouse, Helmsdale. Right *Big
Barns, Strathsteven, Dunrobin*.
Middle above *Dunrobin Castle*.
Above *Golspie Mill*

Oil painting of Dunrobin Castle by William Daniell, c.1822

DUNROBIN

Dunrobin Castle, from 14th century, predominantly from 1841, Sir Charles Barry
A *mixture of an old Scotch castle and a French château* noted Queen Victoria in her journal, an apt description of the vast turreted mansion on a bluff above the open sea, whose core is a 14th-century tower and whose defensive qualities have long been subordinated to picturesque and domestic grandeur. Freskyne's 14th-century tower is still visible, despite continuous additions from the 16th century onwards. Complete transformation of Dunrobin was effected from 1841 when Sir Charles Barry was commissioned to design extensive alterations; by 1845 the 2nd Duke was adapting these designs with the help of William Leslie, leaving Barry on the sidelines in the modern role of *consultant*. They tripled the castle in size with a new entrance in the base of a five-stage tower and the pedimented dormered roofline

In 1785 Elizabeth, Countess, married Viscount Trentham, later Marquis of Stafford, who inherited a fortune in 1803. They expanded their estates in Sutherland until they owned almost all the county. The consolidation of their landholdings, introduction of large-scale sheep farms and consequent *clearing* of tenants to coastal townships are part of Highland history. Much of the present settlement pattern, particularly on the coast, reflects this social engineering. Many 19th-century *improved* farms and estate buildings in characteristic estate architectural style are evidence of a continuous and substantial building programme.

North elevation, Dunrobin Castle. Clock tower and entrance tower roofline, Sir Robert Lorimer

Dunrobin Castle: Above *South elevation.* Right *Stair hall*

The Castles and Pyles of Southerland *are . . . Dunrobin the Earle of Southerland's special residence, a house well seated upon a Mote hard by the sea with fair Orchards, where there be pleasant Gardens planted with all kinds of fruits, herbs and flowers used in this kingdom and abundance of good saffron, Tobacco, and Rosemary. The fruit here is excellent and chiefly the Pears and Cherries.*
Sir Robert Gordon, 1630

Drawing-room plaster ceiling, Dunrobin Castle

dominated by slender conical turrets with fishscale cladding and decorative cast-iron ornamentation. The expensive outcome (£54,663) was the fairy-tale *château* soaring above the formal gardens and parkland, a landmark for ships at sea (colour page 52).

The south garden front survives almost intact, but on the north entrance front the Barry Frenchified roof profile was changed 1915-21 by Sir Robert Lorimer, during fire repairs when the upper stage of the tower became Scottish Renaissance and the clock tower was given an ogee dome.

The main entrance to Dunrobin Castle in the base of the Barry tower leads into a hall decorated with a frieze of the combined Stafford/Sutherland crests; from here a wide staircase, the balustrade fretted with Ss, leads to the main public rooms, mostly redesigned by Sir Robert Lorimer, who created the magnificent 72-ft-long white-painted **drawing room** from two smaller rooms, lit by six tall windows and overlooking the gardens and the sea. The white plaster ceiling and cornice are heavily moulded in Jacobean style (by Sam Wilson) and the two fine classical fireplaces have surrounds of Hoptonwood stone and green marble. Plain wood floors and pale colours were intended as a backdrop for a collection of rich tapestries, glowing porcelain and fine French furniture. Felicitous 1993 redecoration.

The **dining room**, also designed by Lorimer, is oak panelled with a deeply coffered ceiling decorated with vines, an Italianate frieze and Tudor-style fireplace. The **library** is lined with sycamore panelling and shelving with satin-like sheen and the **Green and Gold Room** decorated in French style in 1921.

Terraced gardens are separated from the shore by a high wall with handsome gatepiers and decorative wrought-iron gates. A short rubble **pier**, *c.*1811, served as the castle landing for travellers and goods. The **garden pavilion**, 1732, with square frontage and armorial above the corniced doorpiece approached by a flight of steps, was constructed for William, Lord Strathnaver; greatly extended at the rear in the late 19th century to house the castle museum.

Dunrobin Castle: Top *Carved breakfast-room over-door in style of Grinling Gibbons.* Above *Dining room*

North Lodges, *c.*1810
Pair square, crenellated gate lodges flanking carriage gates. This became the principal castle entrance when the road, constructed *c.*1810, by Thomas Telford, passed to the north of the castle, superseding the earlier route along the seashore. Lodges flanked by stables and carriage houses. *Open to the public during summer months; guidebook available*

Dunrobin Castle policies
Flagstaff Lodge, mid-19th century, probably William Fowler with William Leslie Imposing asymmetrical gate-lodge complex, the carriage and pedestrian entrances flanked by one large and one small circular tower, each

Left *Garden pavilion (museum).*
Below *North Lodges*

Top *Duchess Harriet memorial.*
Above *Sutherland family burial
enclosure.* Right *Dunrobin Railway
Station*

with heavy corbelled and crenellated wallhead. Buildings within the policies include a tall square 18th-century **dovecote**, its circular interior fitted with approximately 500 nesting boxes. A conical **icehouse**, 1786, served as a domestic cold store before the days of refrigeration. Picturesque mid-19th-century **Dairy Cottage** with mullioned windows and gabled dormers, the conical-roofed drum tower (former dairy) crowned with cupola ventilator and weathervane. Contemporary neighbouring pseudo-Alpine **Dairy Barn**, adorned with a first-floor balcony and deep overhanging eaves, was converted for domestic use, *c.*1985, by MacDonald Associates.

A tall, pinnacled Gothic **memorial** to the second Duchess (1806-61) stands in the park. The bust was carved by Matthew Noble and the foundation stone laid by Queen Victoria in 1872 (Duchess Harriet had been her Mistress of the Robes).

Family **burial ground** overlooking the sea incorporates an Italianate pavilion from Trentham, Staffordshire, 1834-42, by Sir Charles Barry, removed after the mansion's demolition. Gravestone to Eileen, 5th Duchess, 1943-4, by Sir Edwin Lutyens.

Dunrobin Railway Station, 1902, L Bisset Mock West Midlands timber framing with rustic gabled canopy. Station opened in 1870 as a private halt for the castle; after many years of closure it was reopened by British Rail in 1985. Bronze **statue** to the 2nd Duke (1786-1861), 1866, by Matthew Noble; though separated by the railway, it was originally intended to close the vista from the north drive.

Kennels, *c.*1860

Handsome ducal canine accommodation. Gabled kennels enclosed by high wall; crowstepped kennelman's bothy with lattice-pane glazing. **Fisherman's bothy**, 1861, George Devey; square grey stone building fronted by a gabled porch with a steep pyramidal roof with contrasting slated banding topped by a louvred cupola.

STRATHSTEVEN & UPPAT

24 **Big Barns**, early 18th century

Crowstepped barn converted as four cottages by George Devey in 1858-9. For inspiration the remodelling draws on the Cotswold vernacular, uses local materials and conveys the impression that the barn is comfortably domesticated. The long frontage was given a short projecting wing at the south-east, with one entry within a deep depressed-arched porch; another gently angled porch grows out of the west gable. Dormers light the inserted attic floor, those with triangular pediments to be repeated on estate buildings throughout Sutherland for the next half-century. But for the name and the tell-tale barn ventilation slits in the east gable, few would be aware of the building's original role nor that a century divided the two building stages. Devey's treatment of the old barn strongly influenced the conversion of the Little Ferry Girnal House a year later (see p.42) and is the stylistic key to the massive estate building programme of the second half of the 19th century (colour page 52).

Top and above Big Barns; *dormers and coped chimney-stacks designed by George Devey, details repeated on subsequent Sutherland estate architecture*

Carn Liath broch, Strathsteven, *c.*100BC-AD100

On the seaward side of the road, just north of Dunrobin. Though only a few feet high (originally as tall as 30ft-40ft) the circular plan is clearly visible. *Guardianship Monument; access at all times*

Brochs are circular, double-skinned towers, skilfully constructed of drystone masonry. They are thought to have been built between 100BC/AD100 as defensive farmsteads, mostly in the Highlands and Islands. Mural cells are built into the base wall thickness, while stairs rise between the outer and inner walls. The single tunnel entrance, sometimes with a massive triangular boulder lintel dispersing the bulky weight of the masonry, is usually guarded by a small mural chamber.

Carn Liath broch

Strathsteven Cottage. Right Uppat House

James Loch (1780-1855) lived at Uppat House when in Sutherland. Commissioner to the Stafford/ Sutherland estates, he was immensely loyal to the family, dividing his great energy and considerable administrative talents between Sutherland and the West Midlands, in addition to serving as a Member of Parliament. A competent amateur architect, he initiated many new buildings in Stafford and Sutherland including a range of *improved* farmhouses and steadings. This he recorded in his book *An Account of the Improvements on the Estate of the Marquess of Stafford* (1820). Much of the stigma of the *Sutherland clearances* was directed against him. Yet he warned Patrick Sellar and William Young, local factors, against ruthless speed in removing people from their homes to make way for more profitable sheep farming.

Inverbrora Farmhouse: Below Datestone with joint Stafford / Sutherland arms (L-R). Bottom Plan, farmhouse and steading, 1820. Right Farmhouse

Strathsteven Lodge, 1864, probably William Fowler
Good example of a Sutherland estate cottage in the Devey manner. Grey stone, gabled centre bay with entrance, sliding sash windows to dormers; the green Cumbrian slate banding is an added decoration to the grey slate roof. **Strathsteven Cottage**, 18th and early 19th century, U-plan, squat and crowstepped, a former *change house* or inn.

Uppat House, from mid-18th century
Two-storey house with wings enclosing the garden front; Uppat has grown comfortably as a home. **Memorial**, 1858, to James Loch (1780-1855); shallow canopy supported by polished granite columns mounted on a bull-faced (stylised rubble) masonry base. Inscribed plaque states that Loch *in the serene evening of his life, loved this place* from which he could enjoy a view of Dunrobin Castle and policies, a view now masked by forestry.

Inverbrora Farmhouse, 1821, George Alexander
Simple, elegant grey Clynelish stone house with symmetrical frontage; corniced doorway in centre recess flanked by wide gables, each with an attic window. The datestone is adorned with joint Stafford/Sutherland arms.

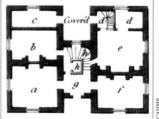

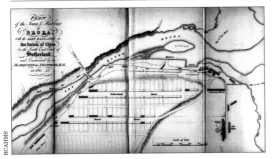

Plan of Brora, 1811-13, from An Account of the Improvements on the Estate of the Marquess of Stafford *by James Loch*

BRORA

Brora has the appearance of a seaside and fishing town, clustered around the mouth of the deep and fast-flowing River Brora. Though the hills are never far away, the small town is set in a broad, undulating estuarine plain, with large farms and diverse crofting settlements, Doll, and Easter and Wester Clynekirkton. Strath Brora is a spacious setting for Loch Brora, more farms and shooting lodges. In the past, with coalmines, saltpans and brick-making, Brora was the industrial heartland of Sutherland. Principal activities are now centred on services, schools, woollen mill, distillery and tourism.

Coal was located at Brora by 1529 and mining started in 1598. From 1811 onwards the Sutherland estate invested heavily in Brora; the mines were modernised, the saltpans revitalised, the coal also harnessed for energy to fire brick and tile works, a brewery and a distillery. By 1872, 5000 tons of coal were mined annually and the brickworks produced 700,000 bricks and tiles. A small power station generated electricity and Brora acquired the sobriquet *Electric City*. Mining continued on and off throughout the 20th century, peaking at 350 tons a week in 1969, closed in the 1970s and landscaped in 1980 as a sports ground; a pavilion stands on the pithead.

The Square

An exuberant cast-iron **Jubilee fountain**, 1897, almost certainly from MacFarlane of Glasgow; baronial **clock tower war memorial**, *c.*1920. **Rockpool**, Rosslyn Street, mid-19th century, pleasant gabled house with large windows and wide bargeboarded dormers providing plenty of light. This was the *Female School*, probably that *endowed in Brora by the Duke of Sutherland where girls are taught to sew, to make their own dresses and other needlework*. **Ardassie**, Harbour Road, *c.*1810, plain rubble three-window front, one of the earliest houses in Brora, formerly a harbourside inn. **Harbour**, 1813, William Hughes, basin enclosed by artificial bank and quay, constructed to export local coal. **Icehouse**, *c.*1830, with round gable, of standard Sutherland pattern.

Three bridges, closely sited in the centre of Brora, span the river: **Old Bridge**, probably 1758; single-arched rubble bridge, replaced in 1930 by Sir Owen Williams' **road bridge**. **Railway bridge**, 1870-1, elegant high single-span viaduct.

River Brora framed by arched railway bridge

Primary School & Community Centre

Primary School & Community Centre, 1962, Allan, Ross & Allan
Originally designed as a secondary school, the building is a typical 1960s block with flat roof and large windows. **Roman Catholic Church of Christ the King**, 1973, by Douglas Reid: simple building in a modern idiom with steeply pitched tiled roof and long windows flooding the interior with light; contemporary church **hall** at rear.

Right *The Terrace. Note S mounted in plaque on gable end.* Below *Bank House*

Clyne Church of Scotland

The Terrace, Victoria Road, 1875
Two-storey dormered terrace of workers' housing built of local brick with freestone dressings: good detailing to eaves and chimney cornices, original rainwater goods and batteries of hand-thrown chimney-cans. Large S for Sutherland on north gable. **Bank House**, former Town & County Bank, 1907, David Horne; pleasant but restrained design, gabled with mullioned windows in grey Clynelish stone. Also in **Victoria Road** is **Clyne Church of Scotland**, 1907, John Robertson. Gabled, pinnacled Gothic: the curved dressed stone window facings of this small grey, buttressed Clynelish stone kirk are characteristic of Robertson's work. The ridge spire was removed in 1945. Next to the church stands the former **Clyne School**, 1903, Sinclair Macdonald.

Sutherland Woollen Mills (Hunter's), from 1874
Brick built, originally constructed as the Duke of Sutherland's Engineering Works and by 1901 run by a Mr Hunter.

Royal Marine Hotel, Golf Road, 1911-13, Sir Robert Lorimer
Marks the emergence of Brora as a seaside and

Beaton

Beaton

Top *River Helmsdale.* Middle left
*Walled garden and pavilion,
Bighouse Lodge.* Left *Kildonan
Lodge.* Middle above *Crofts and
strip fields, West Helmsdale.*
Above *Turf gable and thatch, Strathy*

Beaton

Beaton

Top *Old Manse, Bettyhill (now Farr Bay Hotel).* Middle above *Stafford / Sutherland coat of arms, 1819, Bettyhill Hotel.* Middle below *Balchrick Post Office.* Bottom *Boathouse, Loch Loyal*

Top left *Badcall Bay, near Scourie.* Far left *Limekilns, Ard Neakie, Loch Eriboll.* Middle left *Braeglen, former crofthouse near Achmelvich, Lochinver.* Left *18th-century storehouse, Rispond, Durness*

Below *Calda House, Loch Assynt.*
Middle *Watchtower, Tongue.*
Bottom *Old Church, Balnakeil
House and Balnakeil Bay, Durness.*
Right *Assynt panorama.* Middle
right *Sangobeg, Durness*

golfing resort. Overlooking the river and shore, it was built as a private house named Duncraggie for D H Ackroyd: a welcoming yet dignified dwelling, it has warm brown slate-hung projecting bays and roof, and a Dutch-gabled porch. Entrance hall with original moulded wooden chimney-piece leads to balustraded staircase and wide landing. Later sun parlour. Some of the hotel furnishings came from Andrew Carnegie's Aultnagar Lodge, Lairg (see p.19).

Royal Marine Hotel, formerly Duncraggie

CLYNE
Clynekirkton, former Clyne Parish Church, 1775
Conventional T-plan roofless kirk that astoundingly accommodated 1000 worshippers in its heyday; no wonder the rear wing was added in 1827. Superseded by Brora as the centre of parish worship; closed 1921. The surrounding **burial ground** is tight-filled with tombstones, some graced with fine calligraphy and decoration. Small, circular building with conical roof crowns a nearby mound. Allegedly a free-standing **bell tower**, it looks like an early 18th-century dovecote, stripped of its wall-to-wall nesting boxes. **Balranald**, 1830-40, incorporating earlier house of 1775, is the former manse; the regular five-bay frontage was *a handsome and commodious residence*, according to the incumbent in 1840. Three bee-boles (niches to house straw bee-skeps) in the garden wall.

Top *Bell-tower/dovecote, Clynekirkton.* Above *Fine tombstones in Clynekirkton burial ground*

Clynelish, 1865-6, style of William Fowler
Model farm complex in its time with substantial grey Clynelish stone farmhouse with large canted bay windows and deep-eaved roof in the later 19th-century Sutherland estate manner, part of a fine group which also includes **laundry, cottages, dairy** and large **steading** with a **threshing mill** formerly motivated by steam-power, the boiler fuelled with local coal.

Left *Clynelish farm steading.* Below *Clynelish farmhouse*

Modern still-house, Clynelish Distillery

Clynemilton

Clynelish Distillery, 1819 onwards; the old part with tall brick chimney-stack dated 1820. A seven-block range of bonded stores is dated 1896, each gable set back from its neighbour to form an impressive stepped frontage. The modern distillery complex crowns the rise overlooking the old. The distillery was one of the industrial ventures established by the Marquis of Stafford and the Countess of Sutherland, costing £750 in 1820.

Clynemilton, early/mid-18th century
Two-storey, three-windowed crowstepped house with wide chamfered (trimmed angles) freestone margins surrounding the windows. Later bowed porch.

STRATH BRORA
Gordonbush Lodge, 1871, probably William Fowler
Handsome grey Clynelish stone Sutherland estate shooting lodge overlooking Loch Brora. Gabled with mullioned windows and polygonal turret, the veranda supported by rustic timber columns. The unusual rustic **boathouse**, with boat store in ground floor and first floor with veranda, was sadly burnt down in the 1980s.
Balnacoil Lodge, *c.*1880, perhaps also designed by William Fowler; gabled with unusual slate-hung walls (see also Hope Lodge, p.91) and jettied (projecting) first floor.

Below *Rustic boathouse overlooking Loch Brora.* Bottom *Balnacoil Lodge, slate-hung gabled shooting lodge.* Right *Gordonbush Lodge*

LOTH

Between Brora and Helmsdale the broad undulating fertile farmland of Loth falls gently to the sea from the steep hills north and west. In spring these are golden with gorse and broom, heather clad in late summer and in winter deep brown, perhaps tinged with snow.

Kintradwell is an early Christian chapel site; the much-enlarged farmhouse incorporates the simple *improved* dwelling of 1819. The **Wolf Stone**, 1924, by the roadside at Lothbeg, commemorates the last killing of a wolf in Sutherland (grid reference NC 9413 1001; lay-by). **Crackaig Farmhouse**, 18th and 19th century on site of, and perhaps incorporating, the early 17th-century dwelling said to have been built by Jane Gordon, 12th Countess of Sutherland. The two-storey house has grown over the years, including alterations in 1843-5 by Edward Blore (who worked on Buckingham Palace). Handsome farm-steading range with arched entrance surmounted by Stafford/Sutherland armorial dated 1829.

Parish Kirk, 1822, Archibald Simpson, perhaps executed by Alexander Coupar Handsome rectangular Gothic church with large hood-moulded, Perpendicular traceried windows, carved finials and crocketed bellcote, finely executed in well-tooled masonry. A long Latin inscription records its construction at the expense of the Marquis of Stafford and the Countess of Sutherland. The church was built *after the church at Kintore* [Aberdeenshire] *as your Ladyship directed*, so James Loch wrote reporting progress in 1821.

The circle of society of the better classes in Loth at this period was, perhaps, as respectable as any of the same kind in all Scotland. They were tenants or tacksmen, to be sure, of the Marchioness of Stafford [Countess of Sutherland], but they were more on a footing of proprietors than tenants. They were all, without exception gentlemen who had been abroad, or had been in the army, and had made money . . . the parish of Loth might not unjustly be regarded as an 'urbs in rure'. The Revd Donald Sage, 1806-8

Top *Wolf Stone, said to mark the place where the last wolf in Sutherland was killed c.1700.* Above *Parish Kirk*

Interior, Parish Kirk (1982); note central boxed-in communion table, cluster of columns supporting gallery (partially hidden by inserted ceiling) and cusped panelling

Decorative ogee plaster sounding board, Parish Kirk, Loth

The plainer Kintore church was designed by Archibald Simpson of Aberdeen in 1819 (see *Gordon* in this series).

Though disused, until *c.*1985 the well-lit interior at Loth, planned to accommodate 700 people, retained its rare original layout with long central communion table flanked with benches. The fine fittings included cusped panelled gallery supported by cast-iron cluster columns, holy table, pulpit and elegant urn-finialled, ogee plaster sounding board. Pulpit, sounding board and communion table now at Timespan Heritage Centre, Helmsdale.

The small **burial ground** near Loth Kirk was the site of the earlier church.

Old Manse, 1768-9, later additions
Simple white-harled, two-storey dwelling with regular elevation to the road and sheltered by trees from the prevailing winds. **Kilmote Farmhouse**, dated 1767 but much altered; simple house with steading to rear. **West Garty Lodge**, dated 1863, a plain house of earlier build fronted by a drum tower with porch in base. Mural bee-boles (alcoves) in garden wall to accommodate straw beehives.

Right *West Garty Lodge.* Below *Former inn, Portgower.* Bottom *Former School and schoolhouse*

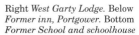

PORTGOWER

A *neat fishing village* in 1855. *Comfortable and agreeably situated* former **inn**, 1813, George Alexander, established to refresh and shelter travellers on the new north/south road passing the door. This is a simple one-and-a-half-storey, three-bay rubble house; rear wing also 1813. The gabled dormers were originally piended; dated Stafford/Sutherland armorial above the door. Gabled old **school** with **schoolhouse**, 1892, in distinctive Sutherland manner (see p.7).

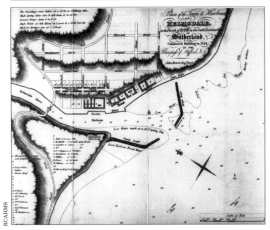

RCAHMS

Helmsdale, plan of 1814

Helmsdale Castle, *a plain looking ruin* in 1858, was finally obliterated by the realignment of the A9 in the 1970s. Long since gone is the early medieval hospice offering shelter to pilgrims on the approach to the tough stretch of road northwards over the Ord of Caithness, to or from the great Nordic shrine at St Magnus Cathedral, Kirkwall (see *Orkney* in this series).

HELMSDALE

The old settlement was sited at the mouth of the Ullie or Helmsdale River where some early 18th-century buildings still stand. It expanded on the hillside above the river as a planned town from 1814 with impetus and investment from the Sutherland estate. The bridging of the River Helmsdale in 1811 was the first step, and from 1814 onwards the curing yards were built, harbour developed and streets laid out in neat grid pattern, soon to be lined with equally neat houses. Streets running north/south have Stafford associations such as Stittenham and Trentham, those east/west after Sutherland, namely Strathnaver or

Beaton

Sutherland Street

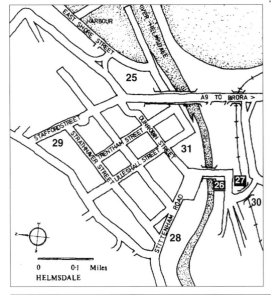

0   0·1   Miles
HELMSDALE

Dunrobin Streets. The development and expansion of the village was intended to give work and to house those evicted from the inland straths, particularly Kildonan. Besides the fishing, new crofts were established in linear plan at West Helmsdale on the southern slopes of the river, their strip fields forming parallel lines on the hillside (colour page 61).

A range of curing yards and the **Customs** 25 **House**, 1818, front the harbour: when built the latter had a salt cellar or store at the rear, salt then taxed. The **harbour** was begun in 1818 and extended in 1823. The roughly triangular basin now in use was built in 1892, by John Barron, engineer (colour page 52).

26 **Old Helmsdale Bridge**, 1809-11, Thomas Telford

Twin arched, it carried the main north/south road over the River Helmsdale until superseded by the 1972 concrete span designed by Babtie, Shaw & Morton as part of the A9 realignment. **Bridge Hotel**, 1816 and later; despite additions the hotel retains its plain but dignified three-window, white-painted front. Large curved gabled **icehouse** by the old bridge, probably that constructed in 1824 at a cost of £100 (rather than the lesser one by the harbour). This is one of the best examples of Sutherland estate icehouses: small walled forecourt and offset doorway to an antechamber which in turn leads to the vaulted ice store. Ice was tipped through the chute at the rear and stored until required for packing salmon for export (colour page 52).

Top *Old Helmsdale Bridge spanning the River Helmsdale, war memorial at left.* Middle *Old Helmsdale Bridge.* Above *Bridge Hotel*

War Memorial, 1924

A prominent three-stage clock tower on the hill above the icehouse. **Church of Scotland**,

27 1908, R J Macbeth; small (former UF) church with spare Gothic detail and bellcote, snug in a sheltered position overlooking the river. **Free**
28 **Church**, Stittenham Street, 1890-2, Andrew Maitland & Sons, a large Gothic successor to an earlier simple building. **Free Church manse**, 1845, conventional three-window
29 fronted house. Former **Church of Scotland**, Stafford Street, 1838; a plain rectangular chapel-of-ease considered suitable for the crofters and fishermen of Helmsdale in contrast to the elegant and expensive parish church constructed for the *gentlemen* of Loth a few years earlier.

30 **Helmsdale Railway Station**, 1871, probably William Fowler
In Sutherland style, gabled with deep eaves and swept roof over veranda supported by bracketed timber arcade, a plainer version of its counterpart at Golspie. Standard Highland Railway lattice-girder footbridge. Helmsdale terminated the section of railway entirely financed by the Duke of Sutherland.

Helmsdale Railway Station with arcaded canopy and standard Highland Railway footbridge

31 **Timespan Heritage Centre**, Dunrobin Street
Occupies an early 19th-century two-storey house. It mirrors and records Highland life and history, part museum complex, part audio-visual displays. *Open Easter-October*

NAVIDALE
Navidale Farmhouse, 18th century and later
Simple crowstepped, two-storey, five-window house sympathetically lengthened to provide more accommodation. Sited in a deep and narrow valley cutting inland from the shore just north of Helmsdale, it was the home first of the Gordons of Navidale and then the Pope family (the latter commemorated in Loth Church). The name is derived from old Norse, meaning promontory dale. A small, circular burial ground, the site of St Ninian's chapel, crowns the headland and overlooks the sea. From Navidale the road climbs steeply to the **Ord of Caithness**.

Navidale, a beautiful sequestered spot nearly surrounded with hills . . . [the house] a plain building, too wide to be a single house, and too narrow to be a double one.
The Revd Donald Sage, c.1800

Navidale, St Ninian's burial ground in foreground, Ord of Caithness in background

River Helmsdale, Strath of Kildonan

Metallic ores are known to occur in small quantities in Sutherland. The most famous is, of course, the occurrence of gold in Strath Kildonan which led to the Gold Rush of 1869. About 500 miners flocked to the diggings, living in a shantytown or under canvas. Gold was found in the Kinbrace, Suisgill, Kildonan, Craggan and Torrish Burns as well as in the main Helmsdale River . . . It is found as dust among the stream gravels, and being heavy tends to concentrate at the base of the gravel against the country rock. It is not known for certain how much gold was found but it has been estimated that £12,000 worth was won in the summer of '69.
Sinclair Ross, The Sutherland Book, 1982

KILDONAN

Helmsdale is at the mouth of the long, broad Strath of Kildonan through which flows the River Helmsdale (colour page 61). The sparsely populated countryside blends into empty uplands and eventually links with Strath Halladale and the Pentland Firth coast. Heavily populated before mass evictions in 1813, the isolated houses are now mostly farms or shooting lodges. Both road and railway follow this northward route to Kinbrace, parting company at Forsinard, the railway line striking out over the moors to Caithness, probably the loneliest stretch of railway in the United Kingdom. Hut circles, cairns and broch sites indicate ancient settlements. **Kilphedir Bridge**, 1820, between Helmsdale and Kildonan; single-span rubble bridge erected, as the heraldic cat and motto *Sans Peur* suggest, by the Countess of Sutherland as part of early 19th-century road improvements. But the name records the medieval chapel site of St Peter (Kil = chapel, Phedir = Peter). There was also a medieval chapel dedicated to St Donan belonging to Scone Abbey at Kildonan, near the site of the present Parish Church, whose immediate predecessor was a *heather thatched popish building*. Unlikely though it may seem, *there is gold in them thar hills!* The discovery of gold in the Strath of Kildonan led to the *Gold Rush* of 1869 when an influx of prospectors arrived in search of fortune; there has been spasmodic gold-panning ever since.

Right *Gold prospectors' huts, 1869, Baile an Or (the hamlet or township of gold).* Below *Old Kildonan Parish Kirk*

Old Kildonan Parish Kirk, 1786-8, James Boag
Small, plain rectangular church, on a lonely site near the river where at least two previous chapels were dedicated to St Donan. Three windows and a doorway in the long south elevation (before 1902, two doors and two

central windows), diminutive bellcote. Interior is dominated by an imposing 18th-century pulpit with hexagonal sounding board and panelled backboard. It was moved from the time-honoured site in the centre of the south wall during the 1902 alterations. Small gallery supported by marbled cast-iron columns. Plaque on east gable erected in 1968 commemorates George Bannerman of Kildonan, whose great grandson, J D Diefenbaker, was then Prime Minister of Canada, and the Selkirk Settlers. Lord Selkirk settled emigrants from Scotland in Canada, amongst them families *cleared* from Kildonan in 1813.

Here, for the 37 years of his ministry in Kildonan (1787-1824), preached the Revd Alexander Sage, whose son Donald, also a minister, recorded this and so many other aspects of 18th- and 19th-century Highland parish life in *Memorabilia Domestica*. Donald's boyhood was spent in the manse, 1766, now **Kildonan Farm**, which he described as . . . *built after the unalterable model for manses in those days . . . with the usual number of chimneys, namely two, rising like asses' ears at either end.* Despite some additions, the traditional two-storey house has not altered much since then. The surrounding fields are enclosed with high-quality drystone dykes.

Kildonan Lodge, 1896, style of William Fowler
Gabled grey Clynelish stone shooting lodge with a complex of **keepers' houses, stables** with mock timber studding in the manner of R J Macbeth, *c.*1900, and a small **school** and **schoolhouse** dated 1883 (colour page 61). Also a somewhat incongruous columned **bus shelter**! **Upper Suisgill Lodge**, 19th century with additions and remodelling, 1988, Lyndall Leet; mid-19th-century dormered rubble cottage flanked by modern sand-coloured harled wings, the substantial new rubble east gable chimney-stack complementing the earlier traditional masonry walling. Designed to

St Donan's, Kildonan. After the evictions from Strath of Kildonan in 1813 the church was virtually abandoned. *During the gold digging period the miners used the church as a sleeping place and provisions were on sale in the gallery. Later a factor used the sacred building as a schoolroom, and latterly nothing remained but walls, going fast to ruin. It is now completely restored and there is no prettier place of worship in the country. The woodwork, in so far as it has survived, is of the wood of the old Caledonian Forest.*
The Northern Times, 17 July 1902

Kildonan Farm sign

Upper Suisgill Lodge

replace **Suisgill Lodge** further downstream destroyed by fire in the 1980s, the new lodge sympathetically amalgamates the old and the new. **Borrobol Lodge**, later 19th-century baronial shooting lodge set in a sheltered valley re-entrant with surrounding cluster of **keepers' cottages**, **kennels** and **outbuildings**.

KINBRACE, FORSINARD & STRATH HALLADALE
Kinbrace

Small village and railway station at the head of the Strath of Kildonan. From here the B871 travels north-west through lonely *flow country* to Syre – surely the largest sparsely inhabited tract of land in Great Britain? Despite its small size, Kinbrace is not without architectural interest. The building materials use for many of the simple houses came in by rail.

Circular sheep fank near Kinbrace; drystone construction with turf cope

Right *Tigh Achen Echen.*
Below *Blar-Mohr, Achentoul*

Dunstalking, late 19th century
Cosy corrugated-iron cottage, probably by Speirs & Co, Glasgow, sent in kit form to Kinbrace by train. The bricks of a **cottage** at the road junction came to Kinbrace by the same route. **Tigh Achen Echen** (?house of the horses' field), 1924. Traditional Sutherland villa, grey Clynelish rubble, probably to a design long extant in the Sutherland estate office by William Fowler. Gabled with canted windows and deep eaves. Railway **signal box** in the garden; modernisation of signalling on the Highland line with EC funding has made these little glazed timber structures obsolete and they turn up in unexpected locations.

From Kinbrace the A897 forges north through Strath Halladale, the route shared by the railway as far as Forsinard. **Blar-Mohr,**

Achentoul, early 19th century, rectangular two-storey house with later additions and remodelling. Neatly harled with painted margins and axial chimney-stacks. Now a farmhouse, it has also served as an inn on this lonely stretch of road.

Achentoul Lodge, *c.*1900; pleasant white-painted gabled lodge with ancillary buildings overlooking a wide expanse of strath and moorland.

Forsinard
Small **railway station**, **hotel** and some **cottages**. **Forsinard Lodge**, probably late 18th century but much modernised.

Strath Halladale is scattered with isolated settlements and small farms, the fast-flowing Halladale River emptying into the sea at Bighouse on the Pentland Firth.

32 **Strath Halladale Church of Scotland**, Craigtown, 1910
This former UF church is unecclesiastical in appearance. A combined corrugated-iron single-storey church and **manse** cheerfully painted with liberal use of royal blue, probably a kit design from Speirs & Co, Glasgow transported as far as Forsinard by train. Long a place of worship, for in 1726 . . . *in Craigtown is a meeting house where the people conveen, when the minr* (sic) *comes to preach to them which is every Lords day.*

Top *Forsinard Railway Station.* Above *Strath Halladale Church of Scotland and manse; corrugated iron with mock timber-studding detailing*

Free Church of Scotland, 1847
Plain two-storey rubble rectangle with a porch at each gable and some original lattice-pane glazing, still in occasional use. Solid **Smigel Mill**, *c.*1850, well constructed of good squared masonry with a regular two-storey frontage, mill wheel, ridge kiln vent and fine local slate roof; built as a local co-operative venture.

Above *Free Church of Scotland.* Left *East elevation and wheel, Smigel Mill*

Crofts fronted by strip fields at Leirinmore, Durness

Beaton

NORTH-WEST SUTHERLAND

The spectacular Sutherland coastline of the **Pentland Firth** seems isolated in terms of road and rail but, until the end of the 19th century and even later, sea transport was the usual and most convenient form of communication. The turbulent waters of the Pentland Firth were an important, if at times dangerous, marine highway, though deep sea lochs at Tongue and Eriboll provided shelter. Well-stocked salmon rivers such as the Halladale and Naver and stretches of lime-rich land were a principal source of wealth.

Durness, the parish stretching from Kylesku in the west to Tongue on the north coast, was owned by the Bishop of Caithness (the see included Sutherland), the Mackay family probably their vassals. This vast area was granted to the Earls of Sutherland in 1559: in 1606 *the Earl of Sutherland yielded to give Durines* (sic) *to* [Hugh] *Macky as a particular fie for his service to the House of Sutherland*. In the 17th and 18th centuries the members of the Mackay family erected houses of some pretension at Bighouse, Tongue and Balnakeil, interesting and unusual survivals contrasting with the majority of later domestic buildings in their vicinity, mainly simple cottages and one-and-a-half-storey houses of the coastal townships (colour page 62).

These coastal settlements were either greatly expanded or established in the first half of the 19th century after the purchase of the Reay estates over a period of years, completed by

Below *House of Tongue.* Bottom *Croft at Strathy including disused thatched cottage (1982)*

Beaton

Historic Scotland

1830, by the Marquis of Stafford and the
Countess of Sutherland. They accommodated
population evicted from inland straths, where
large sheep walks were established. The coastal
settlements reveal both planned development,
where land was *lotted* in orderly strips, and
random growth with crofts squeezed into every
available corner of cultivable land. Strip fields
are easily visible from the road while
innumerable little coastal townships are witness
to the exploitation of nooks and crannies. New
crofts were established between 1900-30, with
the encouragement of the Department of
Agriculture. In these small villages and
settlements one is still greeted by the pungent
aroma of the *peat reek*, the neat peat stacks
mounded near the house. Peat cuttings are dark
scars on the moorland, in early summer piled
with brown cubes drying in sun and wind.

*Melness, cottages in linear plan
occupying* lotted *plots laid out to
receive families evicted from inland
straths in early 19th century*

*Left Eriboll House. Below Heilam
Ferry Cottage, Ard Neakie*

Many townships are reached by narrow lanes
leading from the main A836 and A894 coastal
roads, largely constructed by the Marquis of
Stafford, later 1st Duke of Sutherland, in the
1830s, with chain boats crossing the Halladale
and Hope rivers, the Heilam ferry traversing
Loch Eriboll and fine bridges at Laxford,
Rhiconich and elsewhere. Even as the
landscape also reveals vast barren tracts of
brown moorland and empty straths, deep sea
lochs and green pockets of fertile land, so the
architectural scene is one of contrasts. There
are substantial manses and modern
bungalows, isolated shooting lodges and linear
crofting settlements, small but ancient parish
kirks contrasting with the plain ecclesiastical
buildings favoured by various 19th-century
secession congregations.

Both river and sea fishing provide
interesting buildings, old and new. On the
Halladale and Naver rivers there are salmon

*Fish-handling depot, Kinlochbervie,
1988*

Plan of Bighouse, c.1820

William Mackay of Bighouse
bought Strath Halladale in 1597 for
1000 merks. He lived at Kirkton,
further upstream from the present
mansion, where his son Angus was
born. The move downstream to Tor,
later Bighouse, probably took place
in the mid-18th century. The
Mackays of Bighouse became the
leading cadet branch of the Mackay
family, headed by the Lords of Reay
of Tongue House and Balnakeil,
finally selling the estate to the
Marquis of Stafford in 1829.
Bighouse Lodge ranks with Tongue
and Balnakeil as one of the
important mansions on the
Pentland Firth. The rich salmon
fishings provided valuable income
during the tenure of both families.

Right *Bighouse: Lodge, right;
Barracks, left*. Below *Garden
pavilion, Bighouse Lodge*

stations and icehouses. Small harbours such as
Skullomie near Tongue were built and
exploited for cod and ling. In complete contrast,
in the 1980s EC funds financed the modern
fish-handling depot at Kinlochbervie.

33 **BIGHOUSE**
Enigmatic complex of a large mansion house,
smaller *Barracks*, walled garden and salmon-
fishing station sited at the confluence of the
Halladale River with the sea at Melvich Bay.
The original Bighouse was further up Strath
Halladale, south of Kirkton: no settlement is
revealed on the present site on General Roy's
military survey, 1747-52. South-facing up
Strath Halladale with the river flowing past
the garden, Bighouse stands on a spit of land
enclosed by water on three sides, the site
formerly named The Tor. The anglicised
Bighouse is a corruption of the Norse
bygdhhus meaning village house: the local
pronunciation favours *Begus*, derived from the
early spelling *Begos*.

Bighouse Lodge, *c.*1765, later additions
Severely symmetrical south front with shallow
central pediment, tall chimney-stacks with
flared cornices, early 20th-century continuous
west wing and projecting bowed porch.
Eighteenth-century rusticated **gatepiers** flank
the west entrance to the mansion and
contemporary **walled garden** at the east,
aligned to each other and the small, elegant
*c.*1765 two-storey **garden pavilion**. The
wallhead of the pavilion is decorated with ball
finials while the pyramidal slate roof is
surmounted by a salmon-shaped windvane,
sure indicator of at least one source of
Bighouse wealth. A forestair leads to the upper
room; the ground floor is heated by a small
hearth with simple moulded chimney-piece
(colour page 61).
    At the rear of the mansion there is an
unusual, tall, circular **icehouse**, *c.*1825, with
conical roof built into the side of the cliff.

Barracks, *c.*1730-40

Apparently constructed at Kirkton but probably moved and rebuilt on present site. Low, small, two-storey, U-plan house with small windows tucked closely into the wallhead, corniced ridge chimney-stacks and piended roofs. Re-used 17th-century moulded window jambs surround an off-centre first-floor window, the worn lintel inscribed H MACKAY BIGHOUSE 1738. The building has been subdivided as two cottages and retains no original interior features.

'**Barracks**' can mean servants' quarters; the little house could and would have been relegated as service accommodation. There is also a story, possibly generated by the military-style name, that the rear contemporary store served as an armoury for the Mackays.

Bighouse: Left *Barracks.*
Above *Icehouse*

34 **Kirkton burial ground**

On the west bank of the Halladale River, the site of an early chapel and the home of the Mackays of Bighouse. Affixed to the wall of the burial ground is a carved stone dormer-window pediment dated 1630 with monogram of Angus Mackay of Bighouse. This is probably from an earlier dwelling, superseded by the small U-plan dwelling revealed at Kirkton on Roy's Military Survey, perhaps re-erected at Bighouse.

Above *Kirkton burial ground.*
Left *Melvich*

Four miles west of the church of Rae (sic) is the house of Kirktoun standing close on the west side of the river Halladale (upon which is Strath Halladale) which is the dwelling house of the Laird of Bighouse proprietor of the said Strath.
MacFarlane's *Geographical Collections,* i, 1726

MELVICH, PORTSKERRA & BALIGIL

Melvich Hotel, 1833 and later
Magpie-painted, double-gabled inn with chunky crowsteps in Sutherland estate style.
Portskerra stretches between the main road

Lime kiln, Baligil

and the coast, served by a small harbour. The village and surrounding crofts expanded greatly between 1809 and 1851, from 29 to 100 families owing to evictions (see p.77).

Baligil, small linear settlement; **14 Baligil**, 1889, strange end-of-century-flavoured crofthouse clad in crazy-paving masonry and sporting Gunn family armorial. Here a deep cleft, rich in lime, runs down to the sea with remains of substantial drystone lime kilns: a hill fort crowns the cliff top with dramatic views over the Pentland Firth (see p.3).

STRATHY

Strathy is a small coastal village in the centre of a scattered crofting settlement. From here a road leads to Strathy Point, with panoramic coastal views and lighthouse. Remarkably, the village has four churches.

Free Church, c.1845

Simple single-storey rubble (disused) church with porch added 1881. Gabled **manse**, 1862, small contemporary **school**. The group, though composed of plain buildings, epitomises the strength and independence of the mid-19th-century Highland Free Church movement, constructed and financed by local effort. Close by the **Church of Scotland** (former UF Church) and **manse**, 1910-11, both probably R J Macbeth. The church is a simple building with main entry in south gable under a multi-light window and bellcote. Approached from the east, this seems an isolated group of ecclesiastical buildings, with nothing but moorland surrounding them. In fact, Strathy village is just round the corner, with two more churches. **Strathy Parliamentary Church**, 1828, Thomas Telford, now a holiday home, is the usual T-plan with depressed-arched centre windows, the smaller flanking windows the former doorways (see p.4). The **Old Manse**, also 1828, Thomas Telford, two-storey Parliamentary pattern with greatly enlarged

An eminent Free Church minister of Strathy was the **Revd Hector Macaulay**, 1864-1940. *Born in Gairloch, Wester Ross, where a branch of the Macaulays had long been settled, he studied at the universities of Aberdeen, St Andrews and Edinburgh. In 1889 he returned to St Andrews, from which he had graduated with an MA in classics, to study divinity at St Mary's College. Having declined the offer of the chair of Gaelic at the university, because of his desire to preach in the Highlands, he held charges in Poolewe and Inverness before becoming the Free Church minister in Strathy and Strath Halladale in 1909. Known as the Scholar of the North, his literary output included a Gaelic translation of the Book of Revelations. A generous man, when his wife refused him funds to give to the tinkers he wrote them out a cheque. Mr Macaulay is still spoken of in the parish where he was responsible for the bringing in of piped water to the houses. He is buried in Strathy graveyard where his tombstone wrongly records his age as 74.*
Dr James Macaulay, grandson

Strathy, R-L; former Free Church, manse, church, school, Church of Scotland and manse

windows. The **Free Presbyterian Church**, *c.*1900, a gaunt rectangular kirk lit by round-headed windows.

Strathy Bridge, 1920-30, Sir Owen Williams Unusual bowstring, concrete girder bridge with nine vertical spars; a bold design that stands out well in valley bottom of the River Strathy. **Strathy East & Strathy West**: linear crofts; single- and one-and-a-half-storey houses; some thatched byres with turf gables, here and on the road to Strathy Point (colour page 61).

Above *Strathy Bridge: linear crofts in background fronted by strip fields.* Left *Strathy Point Lighthouse*

Strathy Point Lighthouse, 1958, P H Hyslop First all-electric lighthouse in Scotland. The light is in a square concrete lantern and housing sited within a hollow square affording protection from the elements on this exposed headland. The traditional circular tower was abandoned in order to accommodate more easily the standard electrical fittings.

Before the clearances [*c.*1810] *there had been only four crofters in Strathy and now there were forty-two, over twenty of them from Strathnaver alone; and at Armadale where formerly there were seven, there were now over thirty. Small wonder that their crofts were far too small and had not nearly enough hill pasture.*
Report of evidence given by Adam Gunn before the Napier Commission, July 1883

Bettyhill, Farr Bay, former Farr church (L) and old manse (R)

BETTYHILL
Scattered village on the east bank of the mouth of the River Naver and the ecclesiastical centre of the parish of **Farr** (though in medieval times a priest lived more centrally at Skaill, Strathnaver). The substantial former parish church, occupying an early Christian site, gives some indication of the large local population in

The **Strathnaver Museum** was initiated by Caithness District Council and is now supported by the local community. (For a short period after the 1975 local government reorganisation Farr parish was in Caithness District.) The museum is principally devoted to local *clearances* and crofting life. Also a fine collection of 17th- and 18th-century tombstones, reflecting the status of those commemorated besides the skills of the craftsmen concerned. *Open during the summer; publications relevant to locality on sale*

Top *Strathnaver Museum*. Middle *Pulpit, Strathnaver Museum*. Above *Farr Bay Hotel, datestone with joint Stafford/Sutherland armorials*

the late 18th century; parishioners who lived in the further confines of this far-flung parish may never even have seen the building. The parish of Farr embraces Strathnaver as far south-west as Altnaharra, over 20 miles from Bettyhill, and east along the coast to Bighouse though Strathy and Strath Halladale has been a separate ecclesiastical parish since 1833.

Strathnaver Museum, 1774

Austere and solid rectangular former parish church standing authoritatively in the burial ground beside Farr Bay. White-harled, the south elevation with two long square-headed windows and flanking gallery lights, a similar long centre window unusually at the rear (normally blank). Doorways in east and west gables, where forestairs serve the former galleries. Originally designed to accommodate *750 sittings*, the interior was reduced in size in 1882 by the removal of the galleries. By then the congregation had been decimated, in part by adherence to the Free Church established in 1843 and in part because of the toll taken by emigration. The interior is still dominated by the imposing 1774 pulpit fronted by a reader's desk, the panelled and dated backboard initialed MGM for Master George Munro, minister 1754-79. The title 'Master' indicated that the Revd George Munro had graduated Master of Arts, in his case from King's College, Aberdeen. His tomb is in the **burial ground** surrounding the church.

Ninth-century **cross slab** on the east side of the church has a ringed cross carved in high relief and a background decorated with tight interlace and curvilinear patterns.

Farr Bay Hotel, 1819, ?George Alexander

Simple gabled manse with the gabled porch bearing the *de rigueur* Stafford/Sutherland coat of arms and date. Some of the interior window shutters have been charmingly painted with wild flowers by a wife or daughter of a former minister (colour page 63).

Free Church, 1844

A sturdy plain kirk similar to that at Coldbackie, near Tongue (see p.85). Bellcote topped by ball finial, modern glazing and tiled roof. This was the meeting place of the Royal Commission on the Crofters and Cottars in the Highlands and Islands of Scotland under the chairmanship of Lord Napier, when visiting

Sutherland in July 1883. **Church of
Scotland** (former UF), 1910, style of R J
Macbeth. Plain gabled building whose internal
fittings were provided by Farr expatriates. The
old school (now a field station for the
University of Aberdeen) and **schoolmaster's
house**, 1844, Alexander Coupar; both gabled
with bull-faced rubble walls and heavy
chimney copes: later additions.

Salmon station; sited on slope with
wonderful outlook up-river and seawards. Low
single-storey salmon house and curved gabled
1846 icehouse built into hillside. This was
stocked with ice from a specially constructed
shallow pond. A track from the fishing station
to the shore appears blasted through the rock.

Salmon station, Bettyhill

Bettyhill Hotel, 1819 and later
Many-gabled hostelry which has grown over
the years, the Stafford/Sutherland coat of arms
flanks an internal staircase (colour page 63).
Ivy Cottage, *c*.1830, former Sutherland estate
factor's house, on east side of village. Deep
eaved with bracketed corniced entrance. Heavy
local slate roof replaced with tiles.

STRATHNAVER

The broad, once heavily populated Strathnaver
runs south to Loch Naver. The strath was
systematically *cleared* of population between
1807-22 to make way for sheep farms: two,
Riphail and Langdale (including Syre), were
tenanted and developed by Patrick Sellar,
Sutherland estate factor with William Young,
jointly responsible for these *clearances*.

Some re-population took place when
smallholdings were established in the early
1900s, identified by a series of plain gabled
houses along the roadside. **Syre Farmhouse**,
simple early 19th-century dwelling associated
with Sellar. Neat, tiny late 19th-century
corrugated-iron **Syre Church** with Gothic

*Syre Farm, developed by Patrick
Sellar as a sheep farm for himself
after Strathnaver clearances, c.1815*

35

Syre Church

We and our fathers have been cruelly burnt like wasps out of Strathnaver, and forced down to the barren rocks of the seashore, where we had in many cases to carry earth on our backs to form a patch of land. Now, after we have improved the land, at our own expense, and built houses, our rents are raised at every opportunity always when the head of a family dies and a new name is put on the rent roll.
Angus MacKay, Farr, giving evidence before the Napier Commission, Bettyhill, July 1883

Below *Broch at Grummore, Loch Naver. Though ruinous, the hollow circular plan is clear, the trees growing out of the central void.* Bottom *Loch Naver at head of Strathnaver*

Historic Scotland

windows (probably Speirs & Co, Glasgow, see p.8) stands on the site of a former mission chapel serving a population which stood at nearly 200 in 1806. **Syre** and **Langdale Lodges**; large, gabled and white-harled, 19th-century shooting lodges.

36 Rosal

The appearance of early 19th-century Strathnaver *townships* can be gleaned from Rosal on the west bank of the river, which supported 13 families (70-80 persons) in the first decade of the 1800s and was *cleared* in 1816, excavated in the 1960s under the direction of Dr Horace Fairhurst. The cluster of ruinous, cruck-framed cottages is lucidly interpreted on site by the Forestry Commission. *Open at all times; explanatory plaques on site*

Macleod Memorial; opposite Rosal, on the east bank of the River Naver, a plain rubble memorial bearing the inscription: *In memory of Donald Macleod, Stone Mason, who witnessed the Destruction of Rossal in 1814 and wrote* Gloomy Memories. In fact, Rosal (the spellings differ) was cleared in 1816. Macleod observed the burning and clearing of other townships, agitated against the removal of the townships and continued in this vein after emigrating to Canada. However, no evidence of house burning was noted in the 1960s excavation of Rosal.

37 Grumbeg & Grummore

Grumbeg is a deserted early Christian chapel site overlooking Loch Naver; tombstone with crudely carved cross now in Strathnaver Museum, Bettyhill. A well-defined, if ruinous, **broch** is sited on the lochside beside the **Grummore** caravan park. **Altnaharra** stands at the head of Loch Naver. Grumbeg and Grummore were *cleared* in 1819.

Beaton

Beaton

Beaton

Borgie was cleared in the 19th century for sheep, became a sporting estate and, in 1916, the Duke of Sutherland gifted the 12,000-acre estate to the nation *for settlement of sailors and soldiers who have been on foreign service and who had volunteered without compulsion and have a good record of foreign service.* Ten smallholdings were created, with additional work for the occupants in forestry.
Leah Leneman, 'Borgie a debatable gift to the Nation?', *Northern Scotland*, 9, 1989. Borgie reverted to the Sutherland estate in 1993.

BORGIE, TORRISDALE & SKERRAY
Borgie

Crofting settlement re-established *c.*1919. Six of the smallholdings line the Torrisdale Road: two-storey dormered rubble **houses**, constructed *c.*1920, harking back in style to the earlier Sutherland architectural traditions, with their plain frontages, centre doorways and wallhead dormers. Besides the usual end-gable chimneys, each has a substantial rear stack. The simple single-storey **steadings**, originally thatched, are of characteristic local pattern.

Torrisdale & Skerray

Principal centres of scattered crofting settlements between the River Borgie and Tongue Bay. The **burial ground** on the shore at Torrisdale may be an earlier chapel site. The sheltered beach was once used for the export of salmon and beef, salted and packed in barrels, the coopers working there during the summer months.

38   Corrugated-iron **Torrisdale Church**, *c.*1900, ?Speirs & Co, Glasgow, and a large, gaunt former **school** are the public buildings in this scattered community, while single-storey and one-and-a-half-storey houses provide the usual domestic pattern. There are still a few thatched outbuildings.

Skullomie Harbour, near Coldbackie, another linear settlement, is said to have been built for the use of the people of Tongue. Inconveniently distant, it may never have seen much use. It is of interest for the skilled use of heavy drystone masonry.

Loch Loyal

From Tongue the A383 proceeds south to Altnaharra along the length of Lochs Craggie and Loyal, with wide views of central Sutherland. This highway was constructed by the Commission for Highland Roads & Bridges, completed *c.*1819, principal engineer Thomas

Beaton

Beaton

Top *Skerray Post Office.* Above *Lonely bus stop near Skerray.* Below *Skullomie Harbour, massive masonry*

Historic Scotland

39 Telford. **Loch Loyal Lodge**, dated 1883, style of William Fowler, gabled Sutherland estate shooting lodge with arcaded timber veranda (see p.7) and plaque inscribed with a large S. **Boathouse**, 1993, Law & Dunbar-Nasmith Partnership. Timber, rubble and turf roofed, design, materials and techniques draw on Scandinavian (it houses a Norwegian boat) and Highland vernacular traditions (colour page 63).

House of Tongue

TONGUE

Tongue (Old Norse *tunga*, a tongue of land), a village on the east shore of the deep and beautiful Kyle of Tongue, the long sea loch traversed by ferry until the causeway carrying the A838 was constructed in 1971. Tongue was the domain of the Lordship of Reay, the principal branch of the Mackay family, which dominated Durness and Strathnaver from the 16th century and whose cadet branches spread throughout north-west Sutherland, from Kylesku in the west to Bighouse in the east. *Macky his special Residence is at Toung* wrote Sir Robert Gordon, Historian of Sutherland, in 1630. This *special Residence* was a tower-house, in time superseded by the House of Tongue which has grown and altered over centuries. The Mackays of Reay were in decline by the early 19th century and by 1830 all north-west Sutherland had been bought by the Marquis of Stafford and his Countess of Sutherland.

Tongue was originally in the vast parish of Durness, divided in 1724 into the three parishes of Durness, Eddrachillis and Tongue. There are similarities between Tongue and Durness churches, both chronologically and stylistically. Tongue and Durness kirks both occupy medieval sites and were both re-built in the second decade of the 17th century with subsequent alterations and accretions. The old, main portions with doorways in the centre of long south elevations and with narrow gables with laird's entrances with window above at

West gable with laird's loft entrance and window, St Andrew's Church. Compare with almost identical east gable, old Durness Church, Balnakeil

west and east respectively, are very similar. They are probably the only survivals of the considerable rebuilding of parish churches in Sutherland carried out by Sir Robert Gordon before 1630 (see p.29).

Garden front, House of Tongue

House of Tongue, dated 1678 & 1750
Over the centuries the House of Tongue has grown into a pleasant homogeneous group standing within gardens enclosed by high walls. The main block, dated 1678, is probably the house said to have been rebuilt by Donald, Lord of Reay, after destruction by General Monk's troops during the Civil War (1660-9), and heightened in 1750. North porch, 1841. Tall, plain garden front with raised first-floor entrance and narrow windows, both dates cut on the north-east skewputt. Earlier rear buttressed single-storey-and-attic wing lit by later swept dormers, roofed with heavy local Melness slates in 1841. Part of this wing, served by a narrow doorway and with two squat 17th-century ridge chimney-stacks, dates from the 1620s. Even earlier was the tower-house of Tongue, which stood by the garden wall near the main gates, demolished by 1830. Possibly the decorative Mackay dormer pediments mounted in a room in the House of Tongue were saved from this early tower.

Fine faceted obelisk-type **sundial**, 1714. The principal (west) entrance is from the road through elegant late 18th-century **gatepiers**, but of equal importance was the present back drive direct to the quay, underlining the primacy of marine communication.

Crowstepped 18th-century **boathouse** is said to have housed Jacobite prisoners from the ship *Hazard*, sunk after a naval skirmish in March 1746, just prior to Culloden. The ship was carrying funds for Prince Charles.

Tongue Mains, 1843, (Sir) Charles Barry, his design adapted by Alexander Coupar
Imposing courtyard steading, the tall arched

Below *18th-century boathouse, House of Tongue*. Bottom *Tongue Mains*

centre block flanked by set-back recessed arcades and gabled two-storey end ranges. The building is slated with silvery-grey Melness slates from quarries at Talmine on the west side of Tongue Bay. Above the main entrance is an intertwining SS monogram surmounted by the Sutherland ducal coronet, for the Duke and Duchess.

Above *Entrance arch with dovecote above, Tongue Mains.* Right *St Andrew's Church of Scotland*

*In **Strathnaver** ther are tuo castles, Borwe (Borve) and Toung:- Macky his speciall residence is at Toung, one myle from the place where the castle doth stand. Macky his buriall place is at the chapell of Kirkboll, which is one myle distant from Toung, and is laytelie repaired.*
Sir Robert Gordon, 1630

St Andrew's Church of Scotland, medieval site and core

Sited on a slope overlooking the scenic splendour of the Kyle of Tongue on the ancient site of *Teampull Pheader* (St Peter's chapel) at Kirkiboll (Old Norse: church farm). The chronological building sequence of this attractive and interesting little church appears to be: *c.***1613**, the medieval fabric of St Peter's chapel, together with Mackay burial vault, was repaired and rebuilt for public worship as chapel-of-ease in what was still Durness parish, retaining the east/west orientation in accordance with pre-Reformation practice. The principal entrance (as now) was in the centre of the south front and narrow laird's entrance in west gable. In **1680**, repairs and alterations by Donald Mackay, Master of Reay, including the Mackay loft, lit by a window above (as at Durness). The doorpiece dated 1680 installed (but not in present position). In **1729-31**, substantial renovations and rebuilding as parish church of the newly *erected* parish of Tongue a year or two earlier, probably including north and south aisles. Slate may have replaced thatch at this stage and the 1680 doorpiece relocated in south aisle. **1861-2**, bellcote, paired windows in east wall (lighting pulpit), interior furnishings.

Whitewashed T-plan church, main pointed-headed doorway unusually sited in centre of south wall, flanked by small window. Crowstepped west gable with narrow doorway below a window, the entrance to the *laird's loft* above Mackay burial vault. Third entrance, dated 1680, in south arm of cross wing, of striated red/cream sandstone, probably imported from Munlochy in the Black Isle. The late 17th-century moulding on this doorpiece would have been very difficult on the hard local grey stone used elsewhere.

Dignified late 17th-century panelled gallery fronting *laird's loft*, which until 1951, boasted a fine late 17th-century canopy with carved foliated frieze, supported by four slender columns with Corinthian capitals and inscribed with the Mackay motto *Manu Forti* and monogram. Installed either by Donald, 1st Lord Reay, or by his son, also Donald, Master of Reay, who repaired or altered the church in 1680, it is now stored in the National Museums of Scotland, Edinburgh.

Laird's loft, formerly in St Andrew's Church of Scotland

Left *Old manse.* Below *Tongue Hotel, 1886 wing*

Lundies Guest House (former manse), 1841, probably Alexander Coupar
Tall gabled and crowstepped L-plan house with diagonal chimney-stacks described by the minister shortly after it was built as *his new and substantial house.* **Tongue Hotel**, 1854, Thomas Brown, Inspector of Buildings, Sutherland estates, possibly incorporating the hotel that the estate had refurnished, 1820-5. Plain gabled and dormered east-facing road front with modern sun lounge. The hotel was doubled in size in 1886, the new west-facing elevation rising dramatically from the sloping site, tall and gabled with full-height projecting canted bay: lying-pane (horizontal) glazing gives added interest.

Castle Varrich
Small roofless square tower of unknown date and origin sited on a spur overlooking Tongue. It has been suggested that Varrich was the Beruvik of *Orkneyinga Saga*: whatever the origin of this squat, rubble tower, it commands

I crossed the Kyle of Tongue to an isthmus where Lord Reay has erected a neat octagonal building. J Henderson, *General View of the Agriculture of Sutherland*, 1812

an unparalleled view of the Kyle of Tongue and the Pentland Firth beyond.

Youth Hostel, 1892-3
English Home Counties style in quintessentially Highland sea-loch setting: two-storey gabled white-harled villa with extensive use of decorative red tile hanging on walls. Begun by the Duchess Blair (see p.15) as **Tongue Lodge** but completed after she was widowed and had left Sutherland.

Kyle of Tongue Bridge, 1971,
Sir Alexander Gibb & Partners
Joined to the Tongue shore by heavily bouldered causeway, the bridge is 201 yards long, supported by 17 pairs of stilt-like legs and constructed to withstand the scouring of the river and tide. Before the bridge, crossing was either by ferry or a long detour around the head of the loch. The ferry points are identified by two small **jetties** on the Tongue shore (to suit varying states of the tide) and one on the west at **Achuvoldrach**. On the Tongue shore the hexagonal **watchtower**, *c*.1810, with faceted roof, overlooks the channel. The building was renovated in 1990, Lyndall Leet. The gateway is closed by an attractive re-used iron gate with double S (Sutherland) design (colour page 64). The watchtower gave shelter to those awaiting the ferry, crossing the Kyle of Tongue: the humbler **ferry building** on the west shore at Achuvoldrach is circular and roofless.

Top *Watchtower, former ferry-signal station and waiting room.* Middle *Watchtower gate, the crossed SS for Sutherland but also recalling the Stafford connection.* Above *Melness House and causeway crossing the Kyle of Tongue*

MELNESS
Melness House, *c*.1780; additions *c*.1845
Plain but substantial house built by John Scobie, tacksman, overlooking the Kyle of Tongue. Large L-plan **steading**. By mid-19th century it was the centre of a 70,000-acre sheep

farm. Linear **Melness** village stretches along the coastline, settled originally by crofters displaced from Ribigill, each *lotted* a long strip of land running down to the shore. Silvery-grey Melness slates were quarried at Talmine and are still in use on some cottages and outbuildings. **Church of Scotland**, 1900, former Free Church; plain with lancet windows and gable bellcote.

Above *Church of Scotland.*
Left *Moin House*

Ribigill, *c.*1780, much repaired and enlarged 1815-*c.*1850
Large farmhouse at the head of the Kyle of Tongue. Fine range of farm buildings mainly associated with sheep farming. **Shepherd's cottage**, 1830, designed and built by Alexander Coupar.

40 **Moin House**, 1830
Insignificant-looking cottage on the lonely A'Mhoine uplands between Tongue and Loch Hope, built as a shelter for travellers. This is the earliest known roadside refuge (that was not an inn) in the Highlands. From Tongue, Moin House is clearly visible on the skyline.

Hope Lodge, *c.*1875, William Fowler
Slate-hung, gabled and dormered shooting lodge with arcaded verandas similar to near-contemporary station building at Golspie by same architect (see p.48). **Ferry cottage**, 1830-1, designed and built by Alexander

THIS HOUSE *Erected for the refuge of the traveller Serves to commemorate the construction of the road across the deep and dangerous morass of the MOIN impracticable to all but the hardy and active native to him even it was a day of toil and of labour. This road was made in the year 1830 and at the sole expense of the MARQUIS OF STAFFORD. Those who feel not the delay nor experience the fatigue nor suffer from the risks and interruptions incident to the former state of the country can but slightly estimate the advantages of its present improved condition or what it cost to procure them. To mark this change – to note these facts – to record this date this inscription is put up and dedicated by JAMES LOCH ESQ. MP Auditor and commissioner upon his Lordships Estates and JOHN HORSBURGH ESQr. Factor for the REAY Country, STRATHNAVER, Strathhalladale and Assynt under whose directions this work was executed and who alone know the difficulties that occurred in its execution and the liberality and perseverance by which they were overcome. PETER LAWSON Surveyor.*
Inscribed plaque mounted on gable of Moin House

Hope Lodge

Dun Dornaigil . . . *an old building made in the form of a sugar loaff & which a double wall and winding stairs in the midle of the wall round about, and litle places for men to ly in as is thought and all built of dry stone without any mortar. Its called by tradition Dundornigil.*
Description, 1726, from MacFarlane's *Geographical Collections*, i

Coupar, with worn Stafford armorial; associated with the chain boat crossing the River Hope before the bridge was constructed.

41 **Dun Dornaigil** or **Dun Dorndilla broch**, 100BC-AD100
In Strath More about five miles south of Loch Hope. Impressive broch with a portion of drystone, double-skin walling upstanding and a fine triangular door lintel of particular interest (see p.57).

ERIBOLL, LAID & RISPOND
Loch Eriboll, a long and deep sea loch with the crescent promontory of Ard Neakie pushing out to the middle from the eastern shore, is set in panoramic mountainous hinterland dominated by Ben Hope. The east side is green with natural lime-rich fields, the west a rocky barren coast.

Top *Dun Dorndilla broch, from Charles Cordiner's* Remarkable Ruins, *1788.* Middle *Ard Neakie and Loch Eriboll.* Above *Ard Neakie lime kilns*

Ard Neakie: four large **lime kilns**, *c.*1870
Each pair of two slightly different dates, built into the cliff and fronted by a small jetty (colour page 62). Lime quarries on promontory; more lime kilns on **Eilean Choraidh** nearby. Two-storey gabled **Ferryhouse**, 1831, designed by Alexander Coupar, with a worn Stafford coat of arms above the door. From here the Heilam ferry once plied to Portnancon on the western shore.

Eriboll Church, *c.*1804
Abandoned and lonely *mission church*. Quite plain except for the luxury of a diminutive Gothic apex finial. **Eriboll House**, *c.*1836, incorporating tacksman's house of *c.*1780. Regular two-storey house, white harled with reddish sandstone margined windows (see p.77). Substantial farm steading. On the western shore of Loch Eriboll, the *c.*1830, rubble, twin-arched **Polla Bridge** was financed by the Marquis of Stafford's road improvements.

90 Laid, the high address number indicates how congested Laid has been. Note stony terrain and drystone dyke constructed from field-clearance boulders

Beaton

42 **Laid**
Township created in 1832-5 to settle some sub-tenants from Eriboll and to relieve congested settlements established elsewhere after evictions; for some of the original inhabitants of Laid, this was their second enforced move within a few years. A long defile of single- and one-and-a-half-storey cottages, set on a rugged and rocky coastline; each cottage (many now ruinous or replaced by modern bungalows) and patch of land enclosed by massive drystone dykes constructed of stone cleared from the land to create patches of cultivable soil. A rocky, near lunar landscape, the barren land contrasting with the greenness of the Eriboll fields on the east side of the sea loch. Small gabled former **school & schoolhouse**, 1894, in characteristic Sutherland school style, local rubble, reddish tooled dressings and tall chimney-stacks. **Portnancon pier** and **storehouse**, mid-19th century, the pier with later wooden jetty and the store; now a guest house.

43 **Rispond** is a rare sheltered inlet on an inhospitable coast, a haven for shipping for replenishing and refuge. Delightful group of buildings. The earliest of these is the early/mid-18th-century, three-storey crowstepped **store** with a windvane sporting a salmon (colour page 63). Rispond was mainly developed after 1787 by the kelp and fishing partnership of Thomas & James Arbuthnot, Peterhead, who constructed harbour, houses for manager and ship master, coopers' sheds, salt cellar, sail loft, net room and store houses. One of the wings of the principal house contained the (salmon) fish house.

Beaton

Rispond

About 20 of the natives *of this parish are employed in navigating two sloops . . . These sloops were built in the Bay of Durness, in the years 1788 and 1789. They sail from* ***Ruspin*** *[Rispond], to the herring and cod fishing, in which they have hitherto been pretty successful. Statistical Account, 1790*

Durness is a pretty dry spot, the soil sandy, well peopled for its extent. It lies upon a bed of lime stone which here is found in the greatest abundance. It is considered the best grass and pasture ground in the north of Scotland and it was of old the Bishop of Caithness' shealing or pasture farm.
Extract from 'Description of Reay Estate by an unknown Valuator', 1797, in Angus Mackay, *Book of Mackay*, 1906

Smoo Lodge

At Smoo . . . *there is a cave stretching pretty far in underground with a natural vault above. It is called Smoa* [sic], *at the mouth of it is a harbour for big boats, on the floor of the cave there is room enough for 500 men to exercise their arms, there is a burn comes out of the earth in the one side of the said cave and forms a large and deep pond there, where trouts are catched and then runs out of the pond to the sea.*
MacFarlane's *Geographical Collections*, i, 1726. An early description of the Smoo Burn, which tumbles 80ft through a natural vertical shaft, reappearing in the cave.

Leirinbeg House

DURNESS

Durness, the austere and windswept north-west corner of Sutherland where the natural lime makes for grass-covered headlands skirted by white sands and a botanist's paradise in springtime. Small settlements – **Sangobeg** (colour page 64), **Leirinmore**, **Smoo** and **Sangomore** – dot the coastline, some sheltered, some exposed. At **Sangomore** the linear crofts are laid out around the valley, the cottages fronting the road with strips of arable land stretching behind and in front. **Durness village** developed on the main road, succeeding the kirkton at Balnakeil as the centre.

Durness was church land owned by the Bishops of Caithness and in 1559 granted by the then bishop to the Earls of Sutherland. Until 1724 Durness parish stretched to Tongue in the east and to Kylesku in the south; *But, as one clergyman was not equal to the task of instructing the inhabitants of so extensive a district in religion, and inspecting their manners*, it was divided in three: Durness, Tongue and Eddrachillis.

Smoo Lodge, 18th century and later
Wide crowstepped house said to incorporate the 17th-century house of Murdo Lowe. Lowe was an Orkney merchant who traded out of the geo (inlet) of Smoo and is reputed to have employed local women to carry sacks of meal up the steep track from beach to clifftop in return for an oatmeal biscuit.

Leirinbeg House, 1830, Alexander Coupar
Simple, dignified regularly fronted two-storey whitewashed house built for the Sutherland estate Durness Ground Officer, the datestone enriched with the Stafford arms. It is said that masons who worked on Cape Wrath Lighthouse were at Leirinbeg when bad weather kept them from the lighthouse.

Parish Church, Sangomore, 1844, William Henderson, remodelled 1891
White-harled, plain former Free Church with entry in north-facing gable crowned with bellcote.

Balnakeil

The historic centre of Durness parish, a wide crescent edged with white sands and green fields. The site is a reminder of the primacy of sea transport and the importance of the bay,

albeit somewhat exposed, as a landing place for shipping. Here, too, is the best land in the parish.

Balnakeil Church (old Durness parish church), 1619, north aisle 1692, some reconstruction, including gables, 1727-8 Roofless crowstepped T-plan church with similarities to Tongue church. The oldest portion is aligned east/west in pre-Reformation manner, apparently incorporating the ground plan of the earlier, medieval chapel. As at Tongue there is a near centre doorway in the south wall, flanked by blocked windows. Bellcote, 1619, 17th-century mouldings to west window. The narrow gable doorway below a window is directly opposite Balnakeil House probably the laird's entry, perhaps fitted with a laird's loft in 1692 or in the reconstruction of 1727-8, following the pattern already established at Tongue. Off-centre north aisle, 1692, lit by intersecting traceried window, the doorway graced with late 17th-century moulding.

Armorial dated 1619 with initials D MC, KN and RM and Mackay coat of arms. Table tomb inscribed with the epitaph *Duncan MacMorrach here lyis lo, vas ill to his freind, war* [worse] *to his fo, true to his maister in veird* [prosperity] *and vo* [woe] *1623.* MacMorrach is said not to have been buried in the graveyard because of his service to his master in quietly getting rid of trouble-makers! These services may have qualified him for burial below the *laird's loft.* The stone tomb survives, the loft does not.

Walled **burial ground** with memorial obelisk to Rob Doun (Donn), 1714-78, erected 1827. The inscription is in Latin, Greek, English and Gaelic; 200 years later how many are competent in all four languages? Notable also is joint tombstone to wives of James Anderson, Kealdale (*sic*), who died 1783 and 1790 respectively aged 32 and 25. The virtues of each lady are commemorated in verse in clear and well-shaped lettering.

Top *Balnakeil House, built by the Mackay Lords of Reay.* Above *Balnakeil Church; east gable very similar to Tongue Church*

Rob Doun (Robert Calder Mackay, 1714-78) was born at Altnacaillach, near Dun Dornadilla, inheriting a rich oral tradition of Gaelic music and culture from his mother. He was an illiterate cowherd and drover who composed poetry in north-west Sutherland Gaelic, earning himself the sobriquet *Burns of the North.* His poems were published in 1830: some appeared in an English translation in the *Quarterly Review* in 1831 with a memoir by Sir Walter Scott. His poetry reflects and records 18th-century life in north-west Sutherland . . . :
*Wealthy deer and cattle country
And most rich in corn
Land protected from the tempest,
Sheltered from the storm.*

Memorial to Rob Doun (Donn), Balnakeil Church

Top and middle *Balnakeil House.*
Above *Ruined wheel-house once
servicing farm steading, Balnakeil
House*

The principal amusements [in
Durness] *are playing at the ball and
shinty on the fine sands of
Balnakeil. The whole population
turns out on old Christmas Day and
New Year day, and even old men of
seventy are to be seen mingling in
the crowd; remaining till night puts
an end to the contest . . . To keep up
the tone of the action they retire in
the evening, and mingle in the dance
to the music of the bag pipe,
regardless of the bruises and scars of
the contest.*
New Statistical Account, xv, 1834,
p.96

Balnakeil House, commenced in 1720s,
allegedly completed *c*.1744
Incorporates earlier cellars and perhaps earlier
fabric in the west (rear) elevation, probably of
the medieval summer palace of the Bishops of
Caithness. Important and handsome
crowstepped two-storey, shallow U-plan mansion
this was the *occasional residence* of the Lords of
Reay. It commands Balnakeil Bay and church
from its rocky bluff, like the Episcopal dwelling
it succeeded. The tall rear elevation rises from
the cliff edge; the windows of the first-floor
drawing room looking out over the bay. The
symmetrical crowstepped U-plan south front
reflects mid-18th-century domestic comfort and
elegance; the first-floor rooms are well lit while
the attics have diminutive gable-end lights and
small swept dormers (colour page 64).
Walled garden is dated 1863. The **farm
steading** incorporates the earliest *improved*
farm buildings in the north-west: in 1801 there
were slate-roofed barn and byre besides the
heather-thatched *oxen byre*, a cruck-framed
barn, stables and poultry house. Disused early
19th-century **corn mill** served by a lade
(millstream) diverted from the burn flowing out
of nearby Loch Croispol. Late 19th-century
technology also harnessed power from this lade
to serve the farm buildings. Ruined **wheel-
house** downstream from the mill once housed
a wheel and endless wire rope on pulley wheels
running up to the steading to motivate
threshing machinery and other mechanised
agricultural tasks, the only known detached
wheel-house of its type in the Highlands.
The Balnakeil area is notable for fine
drystone dykes enclosing the fields.

Balnakeil Craft Village, 1939-45
Rehabilitated military encampment of flat-
roofed, white-painted cabins, quite incongruous
in relation to its Highland setting but full of
varying enterprises including hotel and craft
workshops. *Open throughout the year*

Old Manse, 1785-6 & 1830; drawing- and
dining-room addition, 1865
Plain house with mural sundial. Substantial
drawing- and dining-room addition added 1865.
Re-used moulded doorpiece dated 1727
inscribed MMD (Murdoch MacDonald) and *God
sees you.* The Revd Murdoch MacDonald (1696-
1763) became Minister of Durness in 1726; an
accomplished musician, he was well known as

a *most melodious and powerful singer* and as a supporter of the local Gaelic poet, Rob Donn, who composed an elegy in his memory.

Cape Wrath Hotel, Keoldale (also Keodale), from *c*.1835
Typical double-pile north-west Sutherland estate house similar to Melvich Hotel and Scourie; crowstepped gables, diagonal chimney-stacks, black-and-white paintwork. Unusual small circular **walled garden**. Set in green fields on a sheltered site on the shores of the Kyle of Durness, Keoldale was long occupied by the Balnakeil factors serving the Lords of Reay, whose principal residence was at Tongue.

Cape Wrath from Scotland Illustrated *by William Beattie, 1838, graphically portraying the hazards and desolation for seamen in this lonely place*

RCAHMS

Cape Wrath Lighthouse, 1828, Robert Stevenson
Short whitewashed granite tower: attendant keepers' cottages with pedimented doorways. The lighthouse can be reached by ferry from Keoldale and then by minibus or hired bicycle for the 10 miles to Cape Wrath.

Drochaid Mhor, *c*.1834
Gaelic, Big Bridge; a fine single-span masonry bridge over the River Dionard, probably designed by Peter Lawson, road surveyor. Many years later in 1881, Lawson placed an inscription over the **drinking well** further south on this lonely road *as a mark of gratitude and respect to the inhabitants of Durness and Eddrachillis for their hospitality while projecting this road.*

This dread Cape [Wrath], *so fatal to mariners, is a high promontory, whose steep sides go sheer down to the breakers which lash its feet. There is no landing, except in a small creek, about a mile and a half to the eastward. There, the foam of the sea plays at 'longbowls' with a huge collection of large stones some of them a ton in weight but which these fearful billows chuck up and down as a child tosses a ball. Cape Wrath is a striking point, both from the dignity of its own appearance, and from the mental association of its being the extreme cape of Scotland, with reference to the north-west. There is no land in the direct line between this point and America.*
Sir Walter Scott, *Diary*, 1814

Kinlochbervie

KINLOCHBERVIE

The deeply indented coastline between Kinlochbervie and Lochinver has many small settlements, though the area is sparsely populated except for these two busy fishing ports, used extensively by boats from the north-east of Scotland. The scenery is ever changing, always dramatic; deep inlets cut into the coastline, patches of green indicate crofting settlements, islands stud the bays enclosed with steep cliffs. Inland the moors and mountains are dominant, spattered with lochs, cut through with streams and rivers with the high, bare rocky tops of mountains looming above the landscape. The coastal road was developed in the mid-1830s (and much improved in the 1980s) with fine single-arched rubble bridges spanning the rivers at Rhiconich and Laxford.

Kinlochbervie is at the seaward end of **Loch Inchard**, enclosed by headlands and reached from **Rhiconich** by a side road with dramatic views over the sea loch, passing through the crofting settlements of **Inshegra** and **Badcall**. **Inshegra school & schoolhouse**, 1879; Sutherland style, twin to that at Acheillie (see p.28), gabled, dormers with large windows, now a restaurant. At Kinlochbervie houses are scattered around the sea inlet, the harbour the focal centre. Here the European Regional Development Fund has financed improved roads and a modern **fish-handling depot**, 1988, Babtie, Shaw & Morton, with access from both harbour and deeply canopied roadside loading bay.

Crofts, Loch Inchard

Kinlochbervie Free Presbyterian Church

(former Church of Scotland), 1829, Thomas Telford
Standard T-plan 'Parliamentary' plan (see p.4). White harled with dressed stone margins standing in a walled enclosure. The church has two central windows flanked by doorways in outer bays and apex bellcote decorative with stumpy obelisks. Refurbished interior. The two-

Kinlochbervie Free Presbyterian Church (former Church of Scotland)

storey Parliamentary **manse**, also 1829 and sited on a headland overlooking the sea loch, is in a sorry state of repair.

44 **Oldshore More**, **Oldshore Beg** (big & little Oldshore) & **Balchrick**
Townships stretching westwards from Kinlochbervie. Some cottages, byres and stores are crowstepped; the crowsteps, normally associated with an earlier date, are a feature of 19th- and even early 20th-century north-west Sutherland vernacular building. There is a good example at **No 144 Oldshore More**, a cottage which is timelessly traditional in appearance though built after 1905.

Above Balchrick Post Office, brightly painted corrugated iron (see p.8 and colour page 63). Left No 144 Oldshore More

Achfary: Below Black-and-white painted telephone kiosk. Bottom Mural memorial to 1st Duke of Westminster

LOCH MORE & ACHFARY

The A838 branches eastwards at **Laxford Bridge** to follow the River Laxford, Loch More, Loch Merkland and the length of Loch Shin to Lairg. This was a *destitution road,* built c.1850 to provide local employment during a period of particular hardship. Shooting lodges are virtually the only buildings in this lonely valley. The earliest is isolated **Gobernuisgach** *shooting cottage,* so described in 1845 when it was designed by Alexander Coupar. The simple, gabled, shallow U-plan house has hood-moulded windows and lying-pane (horizontal) glazing: it is in marked contrast to the later, grandiose lodges that proliferate throughout the district.
Achfary, a shooting-lodge complex developed from 1853 (dated stables) to 1870s by Dukes of Sutherland and then by Hugh Lupus Grosvenor, 1st Duke of Westminster. A mural memorial to the Duke was erected at Achfary by local people in gratitude for work he gave *to the comfort of many.* **Achfary House** is the usual deep-eaved, tall chimney-stacked Sutherland estate red rubble building. In contrast **Achfary School**, 1953, English rustic, timber-clad gabled two-storey building recalls the Kentish Wealden tradition of recessed ground-floor centre bay oversailed by upper

Above *Laxford Bridge, c.1834.*
Right *Achfary School; English rustic weather-boarding and lich-gate*

floor; lich-gate entrance is equally English, both surprising in their Highland setting. The decorative capital letter W proclaims the Westminster estate ownership of the village.

Scourie

Lies in a sheltered hollow near the inlet of Scourie Bay, the village centred on a short curved street (now bypassed) lined with 19th-century cottages and houses, some crowstepped. **Scourie House**, *c.*1846 and later; characteristic crowstepped former Sutherland estate factor's house built for Evander MacIver, Sutherland factor for approximately half a century from 1846 and author of the rambling *Memoirs of a Highland Gentleman*. Scourie House **steading** and **stables** are of east-coast pattern.

Crowstepped cottages in old part of Scourie

Eddrachillis Hotel, 1835 and later
White-painted old parish manse with contrasting window margins and crowstepped gables besides modern additions. The former **Eddrachillis Parish Church**, 1728-31, bellcote *c.*1839. The building was originally heather-thatched, the roof apparently slated in later 18th century. Converted as house, *c.*1970, the small building still sports the gable bellcote; it stands beside the road a little to the north of the hotel.

Badcall Bay fishing station, *c.*1840
Two-storey range with its own jetty, sited on the shore of one of the most beautiful north-west Sutherland bays, originally incorporating fish-house, icehouse and living accommodation. This complex was described in 1855 as *a large establishment for the preserving of salmon*, a role it continues to play as a fish-farm (colour page 62).

Eddrachillis Hotel and salmon station, Badcall Bay, late 19th-century photograph

ASSYNT

The rocky, loch-strewn Assynt stretches south from Kylesku, a dozen miles or so to the

Coigach (see *Ross & Cromarty* in this series). The scenery has an individual and fantastic quality of rock and water, dominated by the dramatic gneiss stacks of Quinag, Canisp and Suilven, besides the worn sandstone hump of Stac Pollaidh (Stac Polly) in the Coigach: it is bounded on the west by a serrated coastline of headlands and bays and eastwards by the bare mountains of central Sutherland. The main A894 twists its way north/south: from it the coastline is reached by narrow roads, creeping into bays and scattered crofting townships, winding up and down glens, following the shoreline overlooking the Minch and the Western Isles (colour page 64).

Below *Kylesku Bridge*. Bottom *Thatched cottage, Stoer, c.1900*

Beaton

KYLESKU, DRUMBEG & STOER
Kylesku Bridge, 1985, Ove Arup & Partners
A *five-span continuous post-tensioned pre-stressed concrete hollow box* bridge. This dry terminology belies the elegant use of the most modern design and technology of its day to span the Kylesku narrows previously linked by ferry. The handsome curved bridge soars over the waters of the gorge, contributing to rather than detracting from, the spectacular mountainous setting cleaved by a fiord-like sea loch, overcoming yet another age-old natural barrier in the communications network of the Highlands. This is as exciting and innovatory as the pioneer Telford masonry bridges of nearly 200 years earlier, earning a Civic Trust Award in 1986.

Nedd, Drumbeg, Oldany, Clashnessie, Stoer and **Achmelvich** are all small settlements serviced by a tortuous winding coast road between Kylesku and Lochinver.

Those (houses) *of the small tenants and cottars are all built of turf or drystone, plastered on the inside with clay, with the exception of two or three in some hamlets whose western gable has a vent and chimney stalk. Several neat cottages, however, built with lime or clay, are commenced in those hamlets where lots are divided.*
New Statistical Account, xv, 1834, p.94

RCAHMS

'Clapper' bridge, Oldany; a bridge type peculiar to the north-west, utilising stone slabs as lintels

Drumbeg School & schoolhouse, 1878
Sutherland style school with stylised rubble
walling. Former **library**, 1909, donated by
Millicent, 4th Duchess of Sutherland, and
described in the *Northern Times* (4 Nov 1909) as
a *magnificent building* [which] *had been much
needed*. Magnificent, indeed, when contrasted
with the contemporary simple village buildings.
Clashnessie retains its scattered **crofthouses**
and **outbuildings**, some of the **byres** still
thatched. The crofts were laid out *c*.1850.

The **Stoer** peninsula is more expansive, room
enough for a later 19th-century model farm at
Clashmore established by the Sutherland
estate *to show crofters good farming* and
accounting for some estate-style dormered
houses on the headland. Clashmore **steading**
was burnt out in the 1887 crofting riots.

Right *Stoer Lighthouse*. Below
Hermit's Castle, Achmelvich. Bottom
*Hermit's Castle, plan drawn by John
Carlile, 1975*

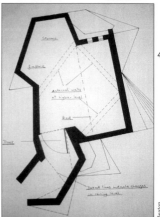

Stoer Lighthouse, 1870, D & T Stevenson
Short circular tower linked to a flat-roofed
block of keepers' houses. Roofless **Stoer
church** and two-storey **Stoer House** (former
manse), 1829, Thomas Telford, are both of
standard Parliamentary church design (see
p.4); the church bellcote is remounted at Stoer
House. A new **burial ground** abuts the old
churchyard, the pink and grey artificial *Fyfe*
stone walling incongruous in this rocky area of
the Assynt.

45 **Hermit's Castle**, Achmelvich, 1950,
David Scott
Diminutive, single-cell massed concrete retreat
sited on a rocky headland at Achmelvich.
Accommodation comprises a bed platform,
hearth and storage shelves, the irregular-shaped
interior never wider or higher than 2m (6ft 6in).
Craggy and sculptural, the strangely stepped,
polygonal form and stark material blend with
the rocky coastline, harmonising both with the
stony Assynt and the stormy Minch spreading
out before it. Designed and built by a young
architect from Norwich, it is now abandoned.

Lochinver

LOCHINVER & LOCH ASSYNT

Lochinver, Loch Assynt and **Inchnadamph** are in the centre of the parish of Assynt which stretches from Kylesku to Elphin, the parish bought by the Earldom of Sutherland in 1757. A sparse, rocky, mountainous area of grandeur but with little good agricultural land except around Inchnadamph (the ancient centre of the parish) where the soil is rich in lime, a commodity once exported by sea from Lochinver.

Lochinver

A busy fishing port, with its large bay a natural harbour fringed with settlements and enclosed by hills. The village of Lochinver was established in 1812, curving around the bay which offers natural shelter to boats with pier and terminal for fishing boats on the south side at Culag. The Highland Stoneware pottery is well established, producing attractive goods sold throughout Scotland. The village also attracts visitors during summer.

Old lime store, Lochinver

Lochinver pier extension, Culag, 1992, Babtie Shaw & Morton. The **Culag Hotel**, 1873, William Fowler; a *commodious mansion*, incorporating the herring station built in 1775 in its rear service wing, now scarcely recognisable owing to repairs after fire damage in 1939. Built as a shooting lodge, it later became a hotel.

Culag House, a former lodge here [Lochinver] of the Duke of Sutherland, was opened in May 1880 as a first-class hotel, with accommodation for 60 guests, and shooting and fishing over 12,000 acres.
F C Groome, *Ordnance Survey of Scotland*, i, 1882

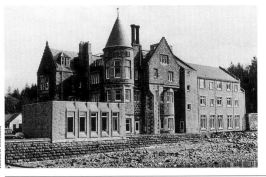

Culag Hotel, built as a shooting lodge in 1873; recent additions

Church of Scotland

The church has stood in Nairn for 52 years, but had been closed for some years and was brought to Lochinver. All facing stones numbered as they stood and the whole taken down and shipped 200 miles round Cape Wrath to Lochinver and re-erected according to original plan. The new building is quite a striking feature when approaching the village by sea or land, its beautiful proportions being very much admired.
The Northern Times, 10 Sept 1903: report of Church of Scotland opening

Church of Scotland, 1903
Former St Ninian's Church of England, Nairn, 1844-5 designed by G Fowler Jones. Dismantled, the masonry was transported from Nairn to Lochinver and re-erected on a rocky outcrop close to the beach under the supervision of John Robertson, who also remodelled the interior. Austere Gothic lit by long lancets, it stands proud in the village.

Single-span **rubble bridge** over the River Inver, dated 1821. Financed by the Sutherland estate, it terminated the road built in the 1820s to Lochinver through Strath Oykel (see p.21). Close by the bridge on the Baddidarroch Road is a low picturesque **cottage** (originally three dwellings) with diamond-shaped chimney-stacks dating from 1845. **Free Church**, dated 1893, D & J R McMillan, low and gabled. The squat square tower has a doorway in base, the upper stage pierced by louvred semicircular windows and crowned with shallow pyramidal roof.

Right *Free Church*. Below *Ardvreck Castle, sketch 1884*

Ardvreck Castle was the seat of the Macleods of Assynt. Here James Graham, Marquis of Montrose, sought shelter after defeat at Carbisdale, April 1650. There was a ransom on his head and he was thrown into a dungeon at Ardvreck, thence bound on horseback to his death in Edinburgh on 21 May. Neil Macleod received £20,000 Scots, apparently in oatmeal which turned out to be sour, and was revenged by the Mackenzie Earl of Seaforth when the castle was besieged, c.1670, seizing control in 1674. Whether Neil Macleod betrayed Montrose or whether he was motivated by a sense of public duty is open to question.

46 Ardvreck Castle, c.1500
Oblong tower and c.1590 turret with associated internal modifications: originally four storeys high, standing prominently on a peninsula jutting out into the loch. The circular stair-tower is corbelled out to square at mid-height and there are shot-holes in the vaulted ground floor. The discerning eye can identify the outlines of **walled garden** and **kilnbarn** nearby, the latter with opposing winnowing doors, the rounded east end housing the kiln to dry corn in the damp Highland climate.

Eddercalda or **Calda House**, c.1725
Sited on the lochside, the roofless shell of the most distinctive house of its time and location. This double-pile, M-gabled mansion house successor to Ardvreck Castle was *built in a modern manner of an elegant figure, and of great accommodation. It had fourteen bedchambers with the conveniency of chimnies*

Eddercalda House (foreground) and Ardvreck Castle on the shores of Loch Assynt with Quinag as backdrop

Eddercalda or **Calda House** was built probably by Kenneth Mackenzie of Assynt, *c*.1725. Brought up in Fortrose, he went to live in the Assynt after his marriage to his cousin Frances. The couple were soon in financial difficulties: according to local traditions there were riotous parties at which the devil was present but their Catholicism would not have endeared them to their neighbours! There were disputes about ownership; on the night of Thursday, 12 May 1737 a party of *weal arm'd men* broke into the house and, after looting the valuables, set it on fire.

or fireplaces, only to be destroyed by fire a decade or so later in 1737. The fact that most of the external walls still stand reflects the quality of building of this substantial house. Calda is one of the first mansions of symmetrical plan and elevation to be built in the north-west Highlands, perhaps *the* first, the style probably derived from Bernera Barracks, Glenelg, 1720-3. Calda was the forerunner of other early 18th-century lairds' houses in the north-west, notably Flowerdale, Gairloch, 1738, and Applecross House of about the same date, both in Wester Ross (see *Ross & Cromarty* in this series) (colour page 64).

47 INCHNADAMPH & ELPHIN

Inchnadamph is a green crescent at the head of Loch Assynt, the land fertile with natural lime. Church and manse identify it as the former centre of Assynt parish. The hotel is a favourite haunt of fishermen.

Old Manse, from 1821, George Alexander Originally a plain gabled two-storey manse now overgrown with additional gabled bay and enlarged windows. The datestone has the Stafford/Sutherland arms of the period.

Old Manse, Inchnadamph, 1821, with later gabled additions, left

Church of Scotland, Inchnadamph

***The Inchnadamph Hotel** is one of
a long line of inns for there has been
some form of hostelry here for over
two hundred and fifty years. The
earliest record is from 1736 when
one Murdoch Mackenzie, a
tacksman / drover, paid 30 merks
and a stone of tallow for the
privilege of keeping a changehouse
at Inchnadamph. The payment of
tallow was common to most
Highland changehouses and inns. A
proper inn was built in about 1780.
Later Inchnadamph became a
favourite haunt of Victorian
naturalists.*
Malcolm Bangor-Jones

The little whitewashed **Church of Scotland**,
1901-3, John Robertson, is low and inviting,
almost domestic in character, with dormer
windows and ridge spirelet. The site is old, the
first church thought to have been built, c.1460,
by Angus Macleod of Assynt, some of which
may be incorporated in the plain, square
mausoleum standing in the walled graveyard.
This is probably 16th century and said to be
the burial place of the Macleods of Assynt and
Ardvreck Castle. The church stands peacefully
in its little walled **burial ground** close to the
shores of Loch Assynt; outside the gate is a
memorial to the crew of an aircraft which
crashed on a mountain nearby in 1941.

Ledbeg, mid-18th century
Simple regularly fronted farmhouse, probably
the earliest still-inhabited house in Assynt. It
was built by the Mackenzies of Ardloch who
obtained a wadset (type of mortgage) of Ledbeg
in 1726 from the Mackenzies of Assynt. They
became substantial sheep farmers but went
bankrupt in 1824.

At **Ledmore** the A837 continues to Strath
Oykel (see p.21) and Bonar Bridge (see pp.15-
17). The A835 proceeds to **Elphin & Knockan**,
more remarkable for scenery than architecture
but the scattered crofts and cottages are
notable for their survival and traditional
appearance. The area was never *cleared* so the
crofting settlement pattern, as at Rogart (see
pp.27-28), is one of scattered, random growth.
The landscape, dominated by the bulk of
Canisp, Suilven and Cul Mor, merges with
Strath Kanaird and Coigach, both in Wester
Ross (see *Ross & Cromarty* in this series).

*Ledbeg, 18th-century sheep farm set
in lonely moorland of the Assynt*

ACKNOWLEDGEMENTS

The author is particularly grateful to Dr Malcolm Bangor-Jones, Laurie Beaton, R I Beaton, Dr Ronald Cant, John Duncan, James G Henderson, Dr Ellen Macnamara, Anne Riches, The Very Revd James Simpson, Geoffrey Stell, The Countess of Sutherland, Professor David Walker and Andrew Wright, all of whom have read and commented on various drafts of this guide. Thanks are also due to all who have enabled her to visit and photograph their properties.

Assistance has also been given by: Catherine Cruft, Ian Gow, Simon Green, Shona MacGaw, Veronica Steele, Ruth Wimberley, RCAHMS; Pam Craig, John Hume and Deborah Mays, Historic Scotland; Helen Leng, RIAS; Dan Ross, Scottish Hydro-Electric plc; M G O'Brien, Highland Region Library Service; the staff of Elgin Library and of Moray District Record Office, Forres; John Baldwin; Gilbert T Bell; James A Blair; Tom Bryan; the late N W Graesser; Jim A Johnston; Willie T Johnston; Donald MacLeod; Dr James Macaulay; John Metcalf, Highland Regional Council; Mrs M Millar, Drumbeg Primary School; Margaret Richardson; Ted Ruddock; David Somerville; Linda Hardwicke, Almond Design; David Alston.

Elizabeth Whitfield has kindly and skilfully executed drawings. Other illustrations would not have been possible without the assistance of the following individuals or organisations: Joanna Close-Brooks; The Very Revd Allan Maclean of Dochgarroch; Highland Maps; Jackie Moran, National Museums of Scotland; Historic Scotland (Crown copyright); Royal Commission on the Ancient and Historical Monuments of Scotland (Crown copyright); Douglas Scott, Elgin Photo Centre; Les Hester, Hester Photography, Forres; Clive Grewcock, Golspie: Michael Henderson, Dick Peddie & McKay, Architects, Edinburgh; James Holloway, Scottish National Portrait Gallery; Scottish Record Office (RHP970/20 Breadalbane Collection, Crown copyright, photograph reproduced by permission of the Keeper of the Records of Scotland with agreement of the Controller of Her Majesty's Stationery Office); Scottish Youth Hostel Association; A J Sloan, Clydesdale Bank plc; Lord Strathnaver for use of Sutherland estate drawings held in National Library of Scotland; Miss C Taylor, Wick Society; Wittets, Architects, Elgin. As is usual in this series the source of the illustration is credited alongside each one.

References

George Devey, Architect, 1820-1886, Jill Allibone, 1991; **Firthlands of Ross and Sutherland**, (ed.) John R Baldwin, 1986; **North Coast Parish: Strathy and Halladale**, Frank Bardgett, 1990; 'The Sutherland Technical School: Pioneer Education for Crofters' Sons', Elizabeth Beaton, **Review of Scottish Culture**, no.7, 1991; **Dornoch**, C Bentinck, 1926; **Studies in Scottish Antiquity**, (ed.) David Breeze, 1984; **Burke's Dormant and Extinct Peerages**, 1883; 'One Man's Castle', Gordon Bryan, **The Scots Magazine**, Feb 1986; **Go Listen to the Crofters**, A D Cameron, 1986; **Exploring Scotland's Heritage: The Highlands**, Joanna Close-Brooks, 1986; **Biographical Dictionary of British Architects 1600-1840**, Howard Colvin, 1978; **Victorian Architects**, F Dixon & S Muthesius, 1978; **The Tyranny of the Tide**, N C Dorian, 1985; **Annals of the Free Church ii**, (ed.) W Ewing, 1914; **The Buildings of Scotland: The Highlands and Islands**, John Gifford, 1992; **Genealogical History of the Earldom of Sutherland, from its Origin to year 1630: with completion to 1651**, Sir Robert Gordon, 1830; **St Andrew's, Golspie**, M W Grant, 1976; **The World of Rob Donn**, Ian Grimble, 1979; **Ordnance Gazetteer of Scotland**, Francis H Groome, 1882-5; **New Ways through the Glens**, A R B Haldane, 1962; **The Architecture of Scottish Post-Reformation Churches 1560-1843**, George Hay, 1957; **The Industrial Archaeology of Scotland ii**, John R Hume, 1977; **Imperial Gazetteer of Scotland**, c.1855; **The Fasti of the United Free Church of Scotland**, (ed.) J A Lamb, 1956; 'Fit for Heroes? Land Settlement in Scotland after World War 1', Leah Leneman, **Northern Scotland**, 1989; **An Account of the Improvements on the Estate of the Marquess of Stafford**, James Loch, 1820; **The Classical Country House in Scotland, 1745-1845**, James Macaulay, 1987; **The Castellated and Domestic Architecture of Scotland**, David MacGibbon & Thomas Ross, 1887-92; **The Ecclesiastical Architecture of Scotland**, David MacGibbon & Thomas Ross, 1896-7; **The Book of Mackay**, Angus Mackay, 1906; **Notes on the Early Church of Tongue**, W J Mackay, 1962; **Telford's Highland Churches**, Allan Maclean, 1989; **MacFarlane's Geographical Collections**, (ed.) A Mitchell & J T Clark, 1906-8; **Scottish Lighthouses**, R W Munro, 1979; **Highland Bridges**, Gillian Nelson, 1990; **New Statistical Account**, c.1835-45; **The Ross and Cromarty Book**, (ed.) Donald Omand, 1984; **The Sutherland Book** (ed.) Donald Omand, 1982; **Tour of Scotland in 1769**, Thomas Pennant, (reprint) 1979; **Scotland, BC**, Anna Ritchie, 1988; **Brochs of Scotland**, J N G Ritchie, 1988; **Memorabilia Domestica**, Donald Sage, 1899; **Statutory List of Buildings of Special Architectural or Historic Interest**, Sutherland, 1984; **Mary Stuart's People**, M H B Sanderson, 1986; **Lorimer and the Edinburgh Craft Designers**, Peter Savage, 1980; **Edwardian Architecture**, Alastair Service, 1977; **The Statistical Account of Scotland**, (ed.) Sir John Sinclair, 1791-9; **George Washington Wilson in Caithness and Sutherland**, John S Smith, 1988; **A History of the Scottish People, 1560-1830**, T C Smout, 1969; **The Waterfalls of Scotland**, Louis Stott, 1987; **The Highland Railway**, H A Valence, 4th edn, 1983; **North Sutherland Studies** (ed.) A Morrison, Scottish Vernacular Buildings Working Group, 1987; **Highland Vernacular Building**, Scottish Vernacular Buildings Working Group, 1989; **The Story of Crofting in Scotland**, Douglas Willis, 1991; **The Northern Times**, Golspie; **Sunday Telegraph**, 17 Nov 1991. Also various local guidebooks.

PICTORIAL GLOSSARY

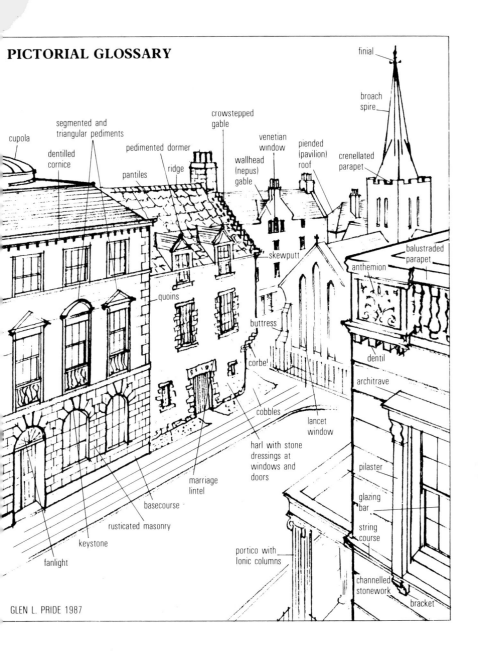

finial

broach spire

crowstepped gable

venetian window

piended (pavilion) roof

crenellated parapet

cupola

segmented and triangular pediments

dentilled cornice

pedimented dormer

pantiles

ridge

wallhead (nepus) gable

balustraded parapet

anthemion

skewputt

quoins

dentil

buttress

corbel

architrave

cobbles

lancet window

harl with stone dressings at windows and doors

pilaster

marriage lintel

glazing bar

basecourse

string course

rusticated masonry

keystone

portico with Ionic columns

channelled stonework

fanlight

bracket

GLEN L. PRIDE 1987

111

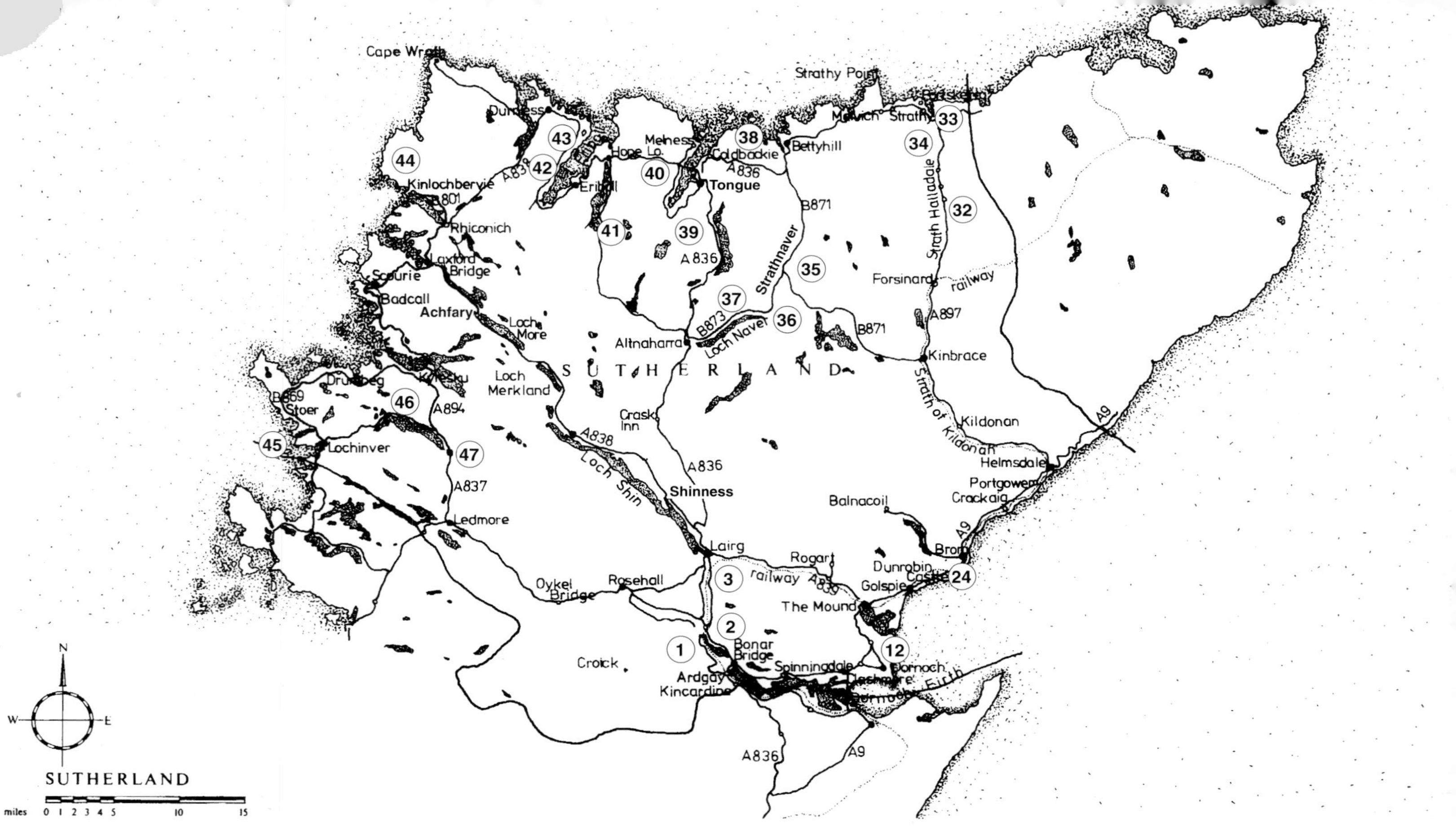
Cape Wrath
Durness
Kinlochbervie
Rhiconich
Laxford Bridge
Scourie
Badcall
Achfary
Loch More
Loch Merkland
Drumbeg
Kylesku
Stoer
B869
A894
A837
A838
A836
B801
B871
B873
A897
A9
Lochinver
Ledmore
Oykel Bridge
Rosehall
Croick
Ardgay
Kincardine
Bonar Bridge
Spinningdale
Lairg
Loch Shin
Shinness
Crask Inn
Altnaharra
Loch Naver
Strathnaver
SUTHERLAND
Tongue
Coldbackie
Melness
Hope Lo.
Eriboll
Bettyhill
Strathy Point
Melvich
Strathy
Strath Halladale
Forsinard
railway
Kinbrace
Strath of Kildonan
Kildonan
Helmsdale
Portgower
Crackaig
Balnacoil
Brora
Dunrobin Castle
Golspie
Rogart
The Mound
Dornoch
Dornoch Firth
1
2
3
12
24
32
33
34
35
36
37
38
39
40
41
42
43
44
45
46
47
N
W
E
SUTHERLAND
miles
0 1 2 3 4 5 10 15